Sharon —

To a life-long friend!
Hope this gives you some hours of pleasure. It's a bit of the past to carry into the future.

Love,
Chris

Merry Christmas
Dec. 1995

*Grandpa,
Tell Me More!*

*by
Stephen Mead*

Editors
Christine Urbaniak, Granddaughter
Teresa VanStratt, Granddaughter

Illustrator
Christine Urbaniak

Reviewers
Delia Mead
Marilyn (Mead) VanStratt
Wallace VanStratt

Special thanks to
Marvin Patterson
Lindell Herrick

*For additional book orders
or for this book on tape
please write to:*
P. O. Box 204
Holt MI 48842

ISBN 0-9644211-0-0
Library of Congress Catalog Card Number 94-90765
Copyright © 1995 by Stephen Mead
Second Edition
All rights reserved
Printed in the United State of America

Memories

Bedtime at my grandparent's house was filled with a sense of anticipation! My grandfather was a superb storyteller! Some of the most special moments of my childhood were spent listening to his stories. I share this gift with my sister, Christine, and brothers, John, Matthew and Gregory. He filled our hearts and nourished our souls!

Grandpa Steve would stand at the foot of our bed and act out each story. His animation and enthusiasm charmed us. He had the ability to capture and communicate his adventures in a vivid and joyous way that brought the past to life and left us feeling his era was a marvelous time to be alive. The tales he described were exciting, inspiring, and funny and through these we learned about his family, community, beliefs and values. His stories reflected a special sensitivity and positive outlook about the world as a wondrous place meant for learning and living to the fullest. His messages made a lasting impression on us. They provided guidance and showed us how to laugh at ourselves. He was a teacher at heart and his excitement and appreciation for life were contagious.

Steve Mead led an admirable life. It is our wish to memorialize his stories with the care and affection they deserve. Our grandparents have passed a rich heritage on to us and we are enormously enriched and proud to be their grandchildren. Our hope is for these stories to touch other lives as they have touched ours.

With fondest memories of Grandpa Steve,
Teresa (Barham) VanStratt, 1995

TABLE OF CONTENTS

SECTION 1: **Introduction**

Chapter 1	Original Script	01
Chapter 2	To My Great Grandchildren from Stephen Mead	03

SECTION 2: **Growing Up**

Chapter 3	Our Family Life	07
Chapter 4	Butchering	11
Chapter 5	Our Family Doctor	13
Chapter 6	Runaways	15
Chapter 7	Earl's Birth Day	17
Chapter 8	Four Boyhood Stories	19
Chapter 9	Christmas at Grandpa & Grandma Chapin's	21
Chapter 10	The Building of the Backhouse	33
Chapter 11	Uncle Leonard	35
Chapter 12	A Train Ride from Albion	37
Chapter 13	When Earl Got Cut with an Axe	39
Chapter 14	My First Stationary Gasoline Engine	41
Chapter 15	The Clarenden Store Fire	47
Chapter 16	The Invitation	49
Chapter 17	Chewing Tobacco	51
Chapter 18	Dad's Steady Character	53
Chapter 19	When Percy and I Built the Cannon	55
Chapter 20	When Earl had the Mumps	61
Chapter 21	The Railroad Ties	63
Chapter 22	Father Could do Anything with a Horse	65
Chapter 23	Butchering the Pig with Ben	67

SECTION 3: **School Days**

Chapter 24	Darrow School	71
Chapter 25	The Curriculum at Darrow School	75
Chapter 26	Hide the Whip	81
Chapter 27	Playing Indian	85
Chapter 28	Trading the Watch	91
Chapter 29	Smoking	97
Chapter 30	Christmas at Darrow School	107
Chapter 31	Preparing for the Michigan 8th Grade Exams	111

SECTION IV: **Grown Up**

Chapter 32	The Car I Built	113
Chapter 33	My Introduction to Grand Haven	115
Chapter 34	Shooting the Bull	117
Chapter 35	Watertown, N.Y.	119
Chapter 36	Hooked at Hawkers	121

Introduction

Chapter 1

Original Script

I have been blessed with a great heritage. The environmental influence of rural life in Michigan in the early part of the 20th century was my lot; it had much to do with my beliefs, habits and ways of doing things.

Our home life was simple, uncompetative, next to nature with close knit family. Our labor-saving divices were few & simple as we had only begun to use fossil fuels for energy. Farm work was done with horses, windmills and manual labor and kerosene & candles furnished light at night for our houses & barns.

I was born December 12th, 1901 the son of Lewis Redfield Mead and Lillian Winifred (Chapin) Mead on the farm taken up by my step great grandfather and great grandmother Blair, moving from Clarendon, New York State, Orleans County in 1835. My great grandfather, Timothy Mead died in 1831 and my Great Grandmother Permelia married Orleans Co. Bennett Blair in Clarendon, N.Y. They moved to Clarendon, Michigan from Clarendon, N.Y. with their three children Chloe, Stephen and Franklin where Great Grandpa Blair built a log cabin they occupied for a year. The second year they built a barn frame house which comprises the main part of the house now standing and occupied by its owners.

cont

When I was a boy I listened to my father and mother grandparents aunts & uncles tell about their childhood. I remember a fraction of what ~~of what~~ they told me. As we had children & later grand children and great grand children, I got the idea I would write my life as a boy. This way I can preserve the way we did things in my generation. The last few years I have been doing ~~doing~~ that.

Stephen Mead

Chapter 2

TO MY GREAT GRANDCHILDREN FROM STEPHEN MEAD

I was born on a farm in Clarendon Township, Calhoun County, Michigan on December 11, 1901. My father's name was Lewis Redfield Mead and my mother's name was Lillian Winifred (Chapin) Mead.

I went to the Darrow school one half mile from home, which was a typical one room country school with eight grades taught by one teacher. In the winter it was heated by a stove in the middle of the room. At morning, noon and afternoon recess we played games, mostly of our own choosing, such as Hide-the-Whip, Pom-Pom Pullaway, Anti-I-Over, Fox and Geese, and Shinney.

Hide-the-Whip was a very popular game in our school. We would all gather on the front stoop of our school and the one hiding the whip would shout "READY!", then all would rush out to find the whip. The one who found it could whip anybody until they got back on the porch again. There was a board fence surrounding the school yard and anyone caught outside the fence often got a flogging. I often wore my long underwear quite late in the spring, anticipating those floggings.

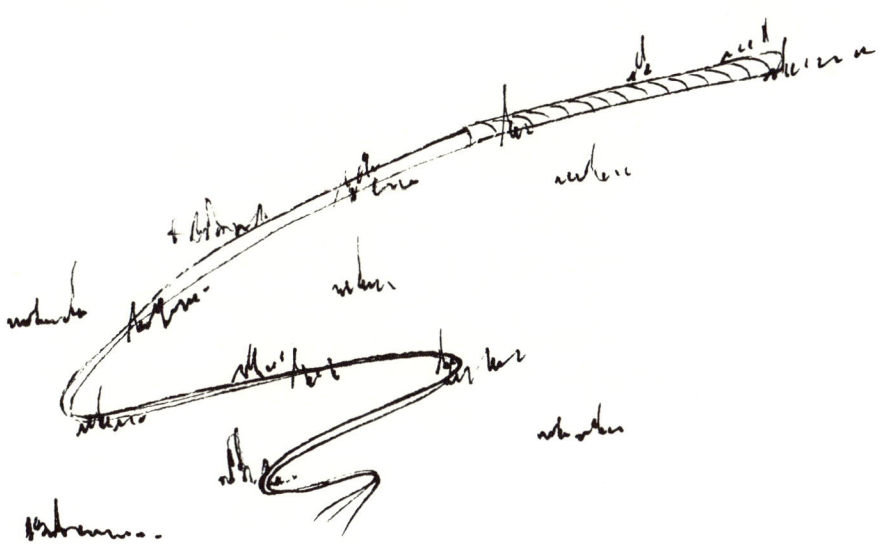

To My Great Grandchildren from Stephen Mead

    In Pom-Pom-Pullaway there were two sides with a lot of space between. One person was "It" in the center trying to tag anyone crossing from one side to the other. When a person was tagged (touched) he or she then had to join those in the center and try to tag those who were still crossing. Soon there were more in the center than those running from one side to the other. The last one to be caught won the game.

    Anti-I-Over was played with a ball thrown over the schoolhouse. Anyone catching the ball had the privilege of sneaking over to the other side and throwing the ball at someone on the other side. If you hit anyone, then they joined your side.

    Shinney was another very popular game in our Darrow school. There was always a hole in the siding in the back of the school building. We had a saying in our school: 'The last one to get their hand in the hole was "it" for Shinney. When Shinney was the game to be played there was a mad rush around the schoolhouse so not be be the last "hand in the hole." Many times the hole would be patched up but somehow it would mysteriously reappear. Then we dug five holes in the ground in a circular layout. The person who was 'It' would take his place at the center hole. It was his job to keep the puck from coming into the center hole and it wasn't an easy job. I was always looking for tree limbs with bent ends to use for Shinney sticks. It was a rough game and I always had badly banged up shins. We weren't delicate with the way we played -- sort of a "country-style" hockey game.

    After I finished at the Darrow school, I went to Homer High School. We lived two and a half miles west of Homer. When it got too cold in the fall to ride my bicycle to school I saddled the horse and rode to town on horseback. I rode with my cousin, Benjamin Wetherbee, and we planned to arrive a little early so we could ride up and down mainstreet a few times to show off our horses. I had a fine Belgian horse and he was a good rider. We kept the horses in the Presbyterian church sheds while we were in school.

    When good weather arrived I got out my Harley Davidson motorcycle. The gravel roads would have been scraped nice and smooth but not like our pavements now. My Harley was a belt drive, one cylinder but had quite a lot of "pep."

    It was an exciting four years at H.H.S. I got to play baseball and football. Our last game of football was played at Union City. We drove over in an open Model T Ford. It snowed and we didn't have any side curtains -- I almost froze. I was a week getting rid of the chill. I was in a number of school plays and I headed up the "Mead's Musical Monsters."

Chapter 2

From high school I attended Western State Teacher's College in Kalamazoo and graduated in two years with a life certificate in teaching and I signed a contract to teach Industrial Arts in the Grand Haven Junior High School.

Now I will tell you when I first saw Delia who has been my wife for 63 years this June. When Delia was 8 years old they moved into our community and John, Nettie, LaVera and Delia started going to our church at Cook's Prairie. John, Dee's father, made her laugh in church so Nettie, her mother, had her sit next to her. After dating in high school, I was paying more and more attention to Dee and on June 25, 1924 we were married in the parlor of the McAllister farm house. We were going to be married on the 20th, Dee's birthday, but it was impossible because I had college exams all day.

In Grand Haven I taught Industrial Arts for 5 years, then I was made Principal of the 7th and 8th grades. A few years later I was made Principal of Central School (kindergarten through eighth grade). I attended U of M summers, was chairman of the Men's Club and received my Master's Degree from U of M in 1938. Two summers I participated in Horn's Flying University, sponsored by Michigan State University and the State Department. One year we visited Industries in the United States. Another year we visited the Air Force Bases within the U.S.

In the summer of 1943 my daughter and I took flying lessons from two different instructors. We were in a race to see who would solo first -- Marilyn or I. We were flying at the Muskegon Airport and Marilyn's pilot took a short cut across the field and she got to 'solo' first. I kept my Pilot's license and flew until I retired in 1966.

Another of my early interests was mechanics. When I was through high school I didn't have a car so I built one out of parts I picked up here and there. It had a Model T Ford block with a Stromberg carburetor and a Bosch ignition system. When it was tuned up it ran excellently. It could outpace most cars on the road. The frame of the body was built out of wood and covered with sheet metal. It didn't have a windshield or floor boards. I finally added these items and put on a top so I could drive in the rain. I had it at Western and the first year we were in Grand Haven. The next year I turned it in on a Model T Ford roadster in Homer.

During the years I was in the teaching profession, I kept my interest in woodworking and built up my home workshop. It has been a great hobby for me since my retirement. I have built many things in my shop but my greatest interest is in the building of clocks -- Grandfather clocks and Mantle clocks of different styles.

Growing Up

Chapter 3

OUR FAMILY LIFE

I have pictured, as near as I can remember, how we lived in those days. Our family life was a very simple life. We carried water from the well which was next to the barn (about one hundred-twenty feet away). We carried it in pails and kept it in the kitchen. We had a wood and coal range which had a reservoir that kept the water warm. When we came with two pails of water, we dumped some of it in the reservoir.

My mother would burn cones from the big pine tree in our front yard and it helped to heat the house on cold mornings. My mother made oatmeal and toast for breakfast and we covered the toast with jam. My mother canned everything -- peaches, applesauce, pears, cherries, carrots and pumpkins. We had a machine that took pits out of the cherries. We did things the hard way, but we got a lot of enjoyment out of life.

Our Family Life

We didn't believe in doing anything on the Sabbath. We were members of the Cooks Prairie Baptist Church. After church and on Sunday afternoons, we spent our time in front of the house in the shade of the trees during the summer meeting with neighbors as they drove by with their horse and buggy. We often had popcorn and apples when they were in season. We had our own orchard producing apples, pears and plums.

When I was a small boy, I must have been in the second grade, I took a stroll back in the woods north east of our buildings. I walked cautiously, for I was in strange territory. My interest led me on because I kept seeing things that were new to me. I finally came to a swale that had quite a bit of water. In it I started seeing scores of red winged blackbirds and I had never seen them before. They were a great attraction to me. I couldn't believe my own eyes. I thought I must be dreaming. It made such an impression on me that I have never forgotten it.

As a boy I had free range. I knew the farmers in our vicinity and I could hunt and go up and down the old St. Joe River as I willed. We had some good times on the river fishing, boating and swimming. In the summer we spent much of our time there when we weren't doing farm work. The river was a big part of my life.

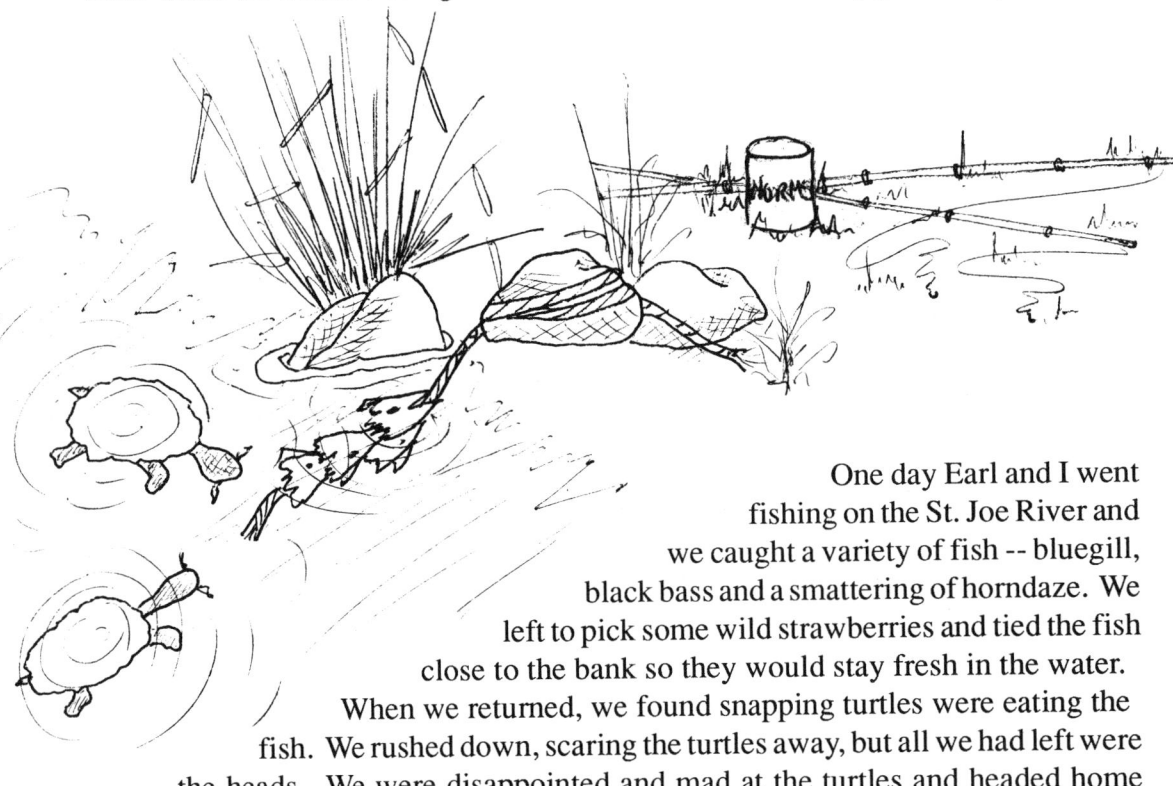

One day Earl and I went fishing on the St. Joe River and we caught a variety of fish -- bluegill, black bass and a smattering of horndaze. We left to pick some wild strawberries and tied the fish close to the bank so they would stay fresh in the water. When we returned, we found snapping turtles were eating the fish. We rushed down, scaring the turtles away, but all we had left were the heads. We were disappointed and mad at the turtles and headed home without our catch.

Chapter 3

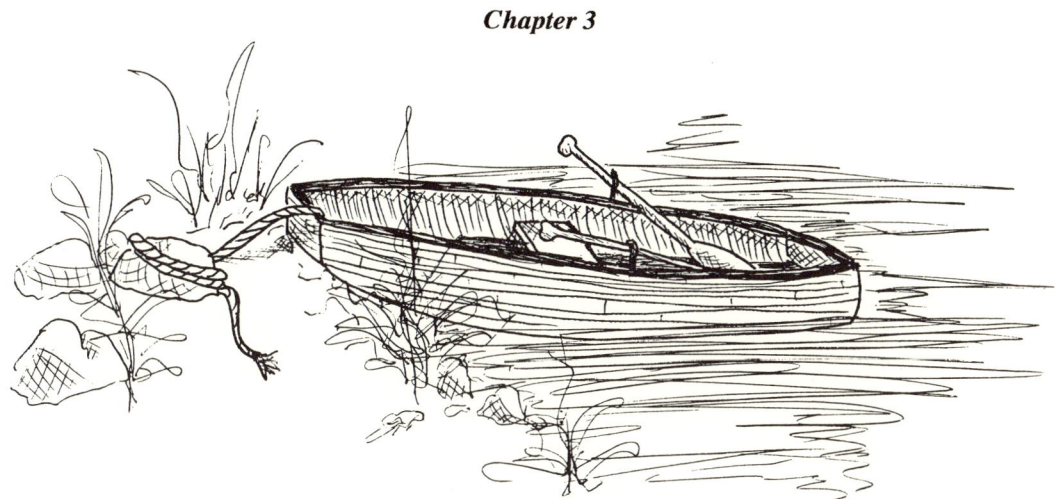

One time when a group of men were stacking wheat in bundles and I was helping Uncle Frank (not my real uncle but a good friend and neighbor of ours). He was talking about a boat he had on the river and said, "I've a good notion to sell it." That pricked up my ears and I asked, "How much do you want for it?" He replied, "One dollar." I said "I'll take it!" It was square on both ends. I fixed it up, tarred the seams so it wouldn't leak and I had it for quite a few years.

I often recall the old swimming hole on the St. Joe River. There was a turn in the river and it cut into the bank making a drop of some twenty feet to the top of the water. We referred to it as the High Banks and it belonged to John Vandenburg, our next door neighbor. A group of boys would gather often forty strong and go swimming "baretail." I must have been close to fifteen years old before I owned a swimming suit (and then I only used it in public places).

When I was 15 years old, I teased my mother and father for permission to have a shotgun. I finally was successful and bought it at Leedle's Hardware in Homer. It was a twelve gauge, single shot. My first time out, I shot a rabbit going away from me and the shot covered his torso. When I picked him up, I had only skin and fur left. I charged it to inexperience.

One time my Uncle Ross Chapin and I discovered some fox squirrels south east of the house. Uncle Ross was bent on shooting one. We got our twenty-two rifles and shot one. He dropped to the ground. We picked him up and brought him to the house. My father saw it and tears came to his eyes and he walked away not uttering a word. My father never owned a gun.

I have fond memories of the old steam engines whistling real early in the morning, as they were sawing logs into lumber. They used these same steam engines during the summer months as they went from farm to farm to do the threshing. The steam engines powered the separator, which divided the straw from the grain.

I went with the threshing gang for two years, pitching bundles into the separator. They changed from steam to diesel Oil Pull (then made in Battle Creek). One day they couldn't get the diesel started. I had gained some experience in college and started the Oil Pull. From then on I was the driver.

When I was going with the threshing gang, we had a man with us by the name of Guy. He was a simple minded man, that could do anything with horses -- break them for riding or harness. He also rode his horse to work. I remember seeing him ride bare back, standing up on the horse's rump and going around in circles.

Guy was a strawstacker and he could build a perfect stack. On one threshing job, we had a basement barn. He put his horse in the basement and built a stack next to the only door. We wondered how he was going to get his horse out. The basement had a narrow width stairway and it must have been fifteen or more steps high. We were amazed as he covered the horses eyes with an old towel and led him up those narrow steps with no trouble.

The family that we threshed for always fixed our dinner or supper. I was sitting at one end of the table, opposite Guy. The phone was above me so I was in a cramped position. The phone was rectangular in shape and hung on the wall. Guy was hot headed and when I said something he didn't like, he jumped over the table and lunged at me. I couldn't go up because of the phone, so I went down. I was in pretty good shape and holding my own during our struggle on the floor under the table until others pulled us apart. I often wonder what happened to Guy.

During the winter they used sleighs to transport walnut logs to make gunstocks during World War I. I can remember the sleighs passing our house during the winter hauling logs (what a waste of time and effort to make gun stocks for a war).

I made Earl a sled so I could skate on the St. Joe River and push Earl along ahead of me. He was all bundled up so he could keep warm. While we were travelling along at a pretty good clip we saw a red fox ahead of us, so I slowed down to a stop and watched him for a minute. He was standing in the middle of the ice covered river and his fluffy tail was blowing in the breeze. It was a pretty sight.

My home

Me

A family gathering

My parents

Earl & Steve

My boat on the St. Joe

. . . with Earl, Nancy (my horse), and Ted

Chapter 4

BUTCHERING

Farm butchering used to be done in the winter time before the days of electricity and freezers. After butchering, my parents would hang the meat in a cold room where it would freeze. Then when they wanted meat to eat they would slice the beef or pork off as they wanted it. A meat saw was used to cut the bones. My father had wooden barrels in the cellar where he would cure salt pork, corned beef and dried beef. At the end of the curing process he would hang the dried beef up to dry. I could hardly wait until it was dry enough to slice off, I liked it so well. I remember when my father thought it was nearly ready, he would get out his sharp jackknife and slice off a piece or two and give me some. My mother often spent a week canning cooked beef in Mason jars.

Butchering

It was a common practice for farmers to do their own butchering, but some hired string butchers to do it for them. My father became so attached to his stock that he hired John Wildt, a string butcher, to do it for him. After the animals were slaughtered, dad would come back home and help with the rest of the work. John Wildt was a tall, strong German who had his butcher knives in sheaths, hog scrapers in good condition, and ability to work seemingly with little effort.

Butchering was part of the food preparing process for farmers, so most of them were well equipped with such things as block and tackle, rope, pulleys, hog scrapers and butcher knives.

We had a big tree between the house and barn with strong stiff limbs. We always kept one pulley, hayrope size, chained to one limb far enough from the tree trunk to give us room to work. By using a high ladder, we would thread a heavy rope through the pulley and draw it through so both ends were even and on the ground.

When we butchered hogs, we had a very large iron kettle we used for scalding them We would place the kettle under the tree near the hanging rope, fill it with water and build a wood fire below and all around it. The hogs, after they were killed, would be plunged into the boiling water a short time, then laid down on sawhorses covered with planks to scrape the hair off using hog scrapers.

We had a horse named Kit who was the most obedient horse we ever had. She would do almost anything on command. After the hogs were killed, we would hook one end of the rope to the hog and the other end to the whippletree fastened to the tugs on old Kit's harness. When the water started boiling, dad would say to Kit, "Gid-dap," and she would walk ahead and draw the hog up and above the kettle. Then dad would say, "Whoa," and Kit would stop. When he said, "Back," she would back up so that the hog would drop into the boiling water. Then he'd say, "Gid-dap," and she would go ahead and raise the hog out. Two men would then pull the hog over on the platform as dad commanded Kit to back up one more time.

If the scalding was done exactly right, every hair would come loose and the hog would be clean and free from hair. The all-white hogs looked especially clean because their skin was lighter.

When the hogs were scraped, the heavy skin was left on the meat. It was called "rind." It was often left on the meat when we made it into salt pork or cooked it. Much of the fatty part of the meat was heated to the melting point and the grease poured into lard crocks and used for cooking before vegetable fat came on the market, such as Crisco and corn oil. After the lard was "tried out." many people put the rind, sliced into strips, in a frying pan and fried it to a crisp. They called it "cracklings."

[As I got older, I did all of our butchering, so this story has a sequel.]

Chapter 5

OUR FAMILY DOCTOR

It was late in August one year when dad decided to sell the wheat. He scooped the grain from the granary into canvas bags and loaded it on the farm wagon. The next day we took it to the Cortright Milling Company in Homer where dad reserved enough to make mother's flour for the year's supply so he could get it as she needed it. The rest was turned into cash.

I have fond recollections of the Cortright Mill. It was four stories high, powered by a water turbine with line-shafts, pulleys and belts throughout the place. The hardwood floors were wax smooth from grain bags being dragged across them. The big exposed beams were covered with flour dust. The grain bags were dumped in an open chute and when the final bag was emptied, a scale weighed the whole load at once. The flour mill had an odor different than any other I have ever smelled and have never found it duplicated.

I recall the trip to Homer with my father as a pleasant one. The horses, Kit and Lady, worked hard to pull the wagon over the dirt roads that two and one half miles. We stopped beside the road a number of times as farmers came out to the road to talk to dad, mostly about farming and politics.

When dad was paid partly in cash for his wheat, we went to the bank and from there to see Dr. Haynes. His office was on the second floor of a building off main street. His office door was open, so we walked in. As we came in, he put his hands on the edge of his roll top desk and pushed his swivel rocker chair back in front of where we sat. He reached up and took off his pince-nez glasses, and inquired how things were going on the farm. Then we got down to the business of the day.

Out Family Doctor

My father said he wanted to settle for the year. Dr. Haynes had no secretary and I assume his bookkeeping was simple. It was purely a one man operation. When he thought about the calls to our family, he put his hand on his forehead in a gesture of rapt meditative thought recalling the times he had been to our house for any illness we had. Finally, he spoke and said, "How would twenty-five dollars be?" My father said fine and whipped out twenty five dollars and paid him. We then had a friendly chat and left as there were others in the outer office to see him.

Chapter 6

RUNAWAYS

My mother signalled for silence as she laid down her knife and fork and listened. We all heard the rattling sound of wagon wheels and the rapid beat of horses' hooves increasing in intensity as it drew near. We rushed from our breakfast table to the window in time to see our neighbor's team running without a driver at breakneck speed past our house. My father started talking to himself, "They're turning in our barn drive. They're going too fast. They can't make it." He was right. They didn't. The wagon hay rack hit the gate anchor post with explosive results filling the air with flying splinters and leaving the wagon hung up on the gate. The impact broke the heavy ash doubletree with a quick cracking sound freeing the horses from the wagon who then ran through the open doors into our barn.

Dad touched the ground only a few times getting to the barn with the rest of us close behind. I was almost overcome with excitement. My shaking knees made standing difficult. My mother covered her lower face with her apron as always when she was nervous. Things looked pretty bad with the twisted splintered wagon draped over the gate post and the perspiring team with broken harnesses standing in the barn. Dad approached the frightened, shaking horses with deliberateness and caution. His low voice, gentle pats on their necks soon had them more relaxed and their ears up.

Runaways

Stillness followed, but not for long. Uncle Frank, naturally slow and deliberate of movement, came lumbering down the road as fast as his large frame would allow. He entered the barnyard gate, tripped over splintered hay rack pieces, then stopped beside the battered wagon, seemingly realizing for the first time what had happened. His hat gone, grey hair down over his eyes, arms hanging straight down, portrayed dejection. Turning to my father, he told what had happened between periods of heavy breathing. "I tied the lines to the wagon rack to get a pitch fork out of the barn and they took off. Something must have scared them." Dad walked over and put his hand on Frank's shoulder. "It doesn't look too bad, Frank. The wagon itself isn't broken so all you will need is a few boards for the hay rack and a 5 foot ash plank for a whippletree." Frank was concerned about his team. "If horses run away once, they are apt to do it again, so I'll have to be extra careful with them from now on." He walked over in front of his two beautiful mares, rubbed their noses and got a friendly neigh in return.

Chapter 7

EARL'S BIRTH DAY

Earl was born January 10, 1908. I had my sixth birthday the previous December 11th. As was the custom in those days, nothing had been said to me about the coming of a baby into our family.

Arrangements had been made for me to go to Lillian Ballentine's to help her bake a cake. I didn't know that the real reason was to get me out of the house. Lillian was my second cousin.

I didn't have far to walk for the farms were adjoined. The Ballentine farm was to the East of us. My father put a heavy coat on me. It was in the dead of winter and a very cold day.

I was happy to be invited to Lillian's to help with the cake. We covered the cake with chocolate frosting and I got to "lick out" the frosting pan.

A few minutes after the cake was finished, my father called me by phone and said he had a surprise for me. I bundled up and headed for home. My father met me at the door and led me into mother's room and I saw Earl for the first time. I was quite taken up with my new baby and I have loved him ever since.

Chapter 8

FOUR BOYHOOD STORIES

  We had some chickens that were hatched in the woods. They could fly almost like a pheasant and we considered them to be wild chickens. Earl and I used to hunt them when we wanted a chicken. We would stalk them in the woods and drop them as they were flying away from or to the side of us. Earl and I had great fun hunting those chickens. The old hens were too heavy to fly, but the roosters could take off and fly almost like a bird.

  We had a tree right next to the road that bore yellow harvest apples. We had a young fellow who drove a sporty car painted red and drove down our road every week. We didn't like the fellow for some reason, I guess because he disturbed our peace and quiet. Earl, Leonard and I picked apples and put them in piles waiting for him to come along. His car made quite a lot of noise and being on a dirt road stirred up a lot of dust, so it wasn't hard to detect his coming. One day he appeared on the horizon and we had our apples piled in bunches ready to fire at him. All three of us started throwing apples at his car and were surprised that he put on the brakes right next to the bank where we stood. He scrambled up the bank and grabbed the first person he saw. It was Leonard, and he gave him a real good flogging. We didn't throw any more apples at his car, but we thought about it many times, as he still drove by all that summer.

Four Boyhood Stories

There was a steep hill north of Clarendon and George Ballentine and I rode our bicycles down it. George would often ride on the bar and I would pedal the bicycle. George's feet were always dirty because he never wore any shoes all summer long. The hill had some bumps in it and it threw George off balance. He caught his toe in the spokes of the front wheel and put a real gash in it. It threw us off the bike and we tumbled to the ground. George was writhing from the pain in his toe. I got George on the bar of the bicycle and wheeled him about 300 feet to his home. I hunted up George's mother, she washed his foot and bandaged it up...which put George on the ill list for a few days. I didn't ride my bicycle down that hill any more.

There was a girl by the name of Dorothy Musser and we were schoolmates. On a cold winter night, with snow on the ground, we bundled up for I was to walk Dorothy home. I had a lantern and we had to go through some woods to get her home. She lived about half a mile from where we lived. As we started going through the woods, the lantern went out, which put us in the dark. We were lost in the woods and didn't know where we were. But, we finally got to Dorothy's house. When I got home, I told my father the whole story; how the lantern went out, our getting lost and finally getting to Dorothy's. My father got a big laugh out of my story, and kidded me for a long time about being in the dark with Dorothy.

Chapter 9

CHRISTMAS AT GRANDPA AND GRANDMA CHAPIN'S

My Grandpa Mead died August 29th, 1886, 15 years before I was born, and Grandma Sarah, whom my grandfather married after my father's own mother died, lived with us until she died in 1918. My father was an only child but my mother came from a large family, so many of our Christmas gatherings were at my Grandpa and Grandma Chapin's in Burlington, just twelve miles from our farm. We often drove it. My father had trotting horses and I recall we used to drive it in about 45 minutes, but a shorter time if the roads were good. They were plain dirt roads, muddy in the spring (at times impassible), dusty in the summer, frozen with deep ruts in the fall and often covered with high banks of snow in the winter. Our buggy wheels, bruised by frozen ruts and stones, had to be reconditioned often by our local blacksmith. Cutters and sleighs were used much of the winter when we had snow.

There were two events each year that I looked forward to with great enthusiasm: Christmas at Grandpa & Grandma Chapins, and family night on George Washington's birthday at the Masonic lodge.

The Christmas at the Chapins that I believe I remember best was in 1910. I would have been nine years old. I counted the days before Christmas for weeks. The day before Christmas, mother spent baking and preparing food to take to Grandma's. There would be a big gathering and lots of folks to feed. Aunts, uncles and cousins; some coming from Grand Rapids and New York, and those who lived near by would come by horse and sleigh. As I think back, Grandma must have been preparing food for days to feed all those who came.

A few days preceding Christmas that year, we had cold weather and lots of drifting snow. There were no radios then and the newspapers were two or three days late, so the only weather predictors we had were my dad and the neighbors (who were a pretty good judge of Michigan weather).

Dad woke up Christmas morning around 5:30, as usual. Every morning he opened all the doors and let the wind blow through the house, then he built a fire in the heating stove in the parlor and one in the kitchen range, then closed the house doors. I was awake, waiting for the house to warm to dress, when I heard our neighbor, Frank Vandenburg, open the door and speak to dad. "My thermometer

Christmas at Grandpa and Grandma Chapin's

reads 5 below. What's your's read?" "5 below here, too," says dad, "so that must be right." "Not going to Chapins today, are you Lew?" "Haven't thought about not going," came the answer as Uncle Frank left.

The house was soon warm and mother was up surveying the situation. As I dressed in front of the stove, I could tell that mother was worried. She said, "Lew, you're not starting out in weather like this." Dad looked at mother with a questioned look and didn't answer (which was quite typical of him in such circumstances). I was depressed over the thought we might not go to Grandma's for Christmas. Mother talked to dad about what would happen if we got stuck in a snowbank with Earl, who was not quite three years old. That worried me, but I had great faith in my dad and I knew if he decided to go I had no worries.

Mother went about her work getting breakfast and food ready to take. Dad went to the barn to do chores and I went with him, dressed in wool underwear, wool shirt and socks, felt boots, fur cap, with a scarf around my neck and ears. I helped feed the cows and horses. Dad took special care of the horses, giving them a big feeding of oats and timothy hay, then led them out for water. Earlier in the morning he had built a pine-wood fire in the horse tank heater to melt the ice and warm the water, but it hadn't had time to thaw the ice, so dad had to chop the ice so the horses could drink.

It was warm in the barn, insulated with tons of hay and the heat from the animals. My shepherd dog, Ted, had a heavy coat of fur, but he didn't venture out of the barn, it was so cold outside. I stayed with dad until he had the stock fed and milking done.

Chapter 9

As we came in the house with the milk, mother had the cream separator ready in the corner of the kitchen, and we started pouring milk in the tank above it. Then dad, with his powerful arms, grabbed the crank and had it up to speed in a short time, and turned it over to me to keep it going. It was hard work for me, but I could do it for a spell.

Mother had buckwheat pancakes stacked, so we sat down to eat before we slopped the hogs with the separated milk. At breakfast, little was said while mother and I wondered what the decision on dad's part would be about going to Grandpa and Grandma Chapins. Breakfast finished, dad bundled up and started down the road for Uncle Ed Ballentine's. Aunt Florence Ballentine was Uncle Ed's wife and my mother's sister, living on a farm bordering ours, and they, too, went to the Chapins for Christmas. Dad came back in about 20 minutes and announced, "We're all going together using Ed's sleigh with his stock rack and our horses." Dad got out the soapstones and had mother put them on the kitchen range with a suggestion to keep the fire hot. Mother started hunting up robes and blankets and warm clothes.

As dad started for the barn, I started to put on my winter clothes, when mother said, "You stay in here and keep warm." I looked at dad, I suppose with that silent language you use in situations like this when mother said, "Do you think he ought to go out there when its so cold?" My dad never said no. It wasn't in his vocabulary. He either said yes or nothing. This time he said, "I'll watch him." I was glad for his consent, because I was eager to be where the action was.

We harnessed Maud & Trilby, the fastest trotting horses in the neighborhood. Trilby was a high strung, beautiful horse. Maud was tireless, an easy keeper and the orneriest horse I ever knew. As a team they were well matched, pulled together beautifully, and seemed to be at their height of enjoyment when they were trotting pulling a buggy or a sleigh. Dad was the only person who could handle Maud and he was a master at it. She responded to his every movement and word. Dad had them harnessed in no time, and we drove them to Uncle Ed's with dad being pulled along by the reins until his steps were long behind two prancing beauties early on a very, very cold Christmas morning.

When we got to Uncle Ed's, he had the sleigh ready with the stock rack up covered with binder canvas, making it almost wind tight. The hay rack on the sleigh was about four feet wide and sixteen feet long, giving us room for everyone to ride. On top of the rack was a spring seat wide enough for two people in heavy coats to sit and drive the team. Uncle Ed had lots of straw in the bottom of the box covered with canvas to make it softer to sit on.

My cousin, Theron Ballentine, was 17 years old. He was dressed in the latest fashion with a black wool overcoat and a derby hat. He declared his intention of

Christmas at Grandpa and Grandma Chapin's

riding beside my father on the stock rack seat. My father, dressed in quite a few layers of wool, with a buffalo fur coat that came to his ankles, buffalo fur cap and mittens and felt boots said to Theron, "Theron, you will have to get some warmer clothes if you ride up there." Theron thought he would be alright, so nothing more was said, and Theron rode the twelve miles on the (stagecoach) high seat with dad, sharing the heavy robe, but with Theron's ears (which were large to begin with) sticking out under his derby hat to catch all the frigid air.

The last thing dad and Uncle Ed did before starting out was to put all the soapstones on the canvas over the straw and cover them with heavy blankets. Dad finally had to climb up on the high seat to hold the horses as they were getting cold and raring to go. Dad drove up to the back door of Balentine's house and Uncle Ed cupped his hands to his mouth and whistled for Aunt Florence, Lillie and Marie to come out and get in the sleigh. They were in the sleigh in nothing flat and covered with warm blankets. Theron climbed up on the high seat with dad and covered his legs with the buffalo robe dad shared with him. Uncle Ed jumped on the back as dad relaxed the reins and spoke to the horses and we were on our way to our house less than a quarter of a mile away. I saw mother, my sister Mary and Grandma Sarah watching us from the window as we drove in our driveway. Mother had everything ready, clothes laid out, food in baskets and Earl wrapped up for Uncle Ed to carry to the sleigh. Grandma Sarah was a large woman and older and needed help to get in over the tail-board of the sleigh. Mary waded through the deep snow with overshoes over her high button shoes, her head wrapped in a scarf and, in spite of youthful vigor, had difficulty getting over the tailgate because of her long full skirt. Mother, with her slender agility, had no trouble getting in and soon everyone was covered with blankets warmed by the soapstones and protected from the snow and wind by the canvas cover over the stock rack. With everyone in place, Ed called to dad that we were ready. Then we sensed the movement of the sleigh and the turn as we entered the road.

Chapter 9

The sleigh tracks were good as the road had been used for sleighing for weeks, making it easy for the sleigh to be pulled. Now and then we ran into deep snow that had drifted during the night and the horses had to work hard to pull us through. I remember peeking out a hole in the canvas watching the wood smoke from the chimneys of the farm houses as we passed. The cold snow squeaked under the sleigh runners and I could hear the horses breathing hard with the breath from their nostrils looking like smoke from a steam locomotive as it hit the frigid air. The ride wasn't smooth. The sleigh had no springs and the sleigh often had a rolling motion as we slid over the drifts. Marie complained of being sick and Aunt Florence sensed the situation just in time to get her to the back of the sleigh and her head over the backboard before she threw up. She left her mark on the white snow at a number of intervals before we reached the Chapin farm.

As we drove in the Chapin yard at Burlington, the cherry orchard north of the house was covered with frost. Grandpa had the American Flag flying in front of the house as always. Dad reined the horses so as to bring the sleigh up to the end of the board walk freshly cleaned of snow. The board walk had a hitching post at the end away from the house. The walk led into the big room of the farm house that contained both kitchen and dining areas.

As we crawled out from under the blankets and out of the sleigh, we were warmly greeted by our aunts, uncles and cousins with the usual hugging and kissing that takes place after not seeing each other for a time. We scurried into the house and were met with the smell of things cooking on the big kitchen range.

Grandpa Chapin walked around the horses observing their heads held high, heavy breathing and bodies covered with lather from the heavy perspiration. He raised the collars from their shoulders and with his other hand wiped the moisture from their withers, then looked up at dad and said, "I've got the stalls ready. We better get them inside right away and rub them down." The sleigh unloaded, dad and grandpa drove in the barn across the road. It was then that grandpa noticed Theron on the seat beside dad with his derby hat on and ears exposed. With a concerned look, grandpa said, "Theron, you better get inside before you freeze through."

As we entered the house, we found Uncle Leonard, grandpa's bachelor brother sitting by the kitchen range. He was a Civil War veteran and lived with Grandpa and Grandpa Chapin until he died. He had just finished his part of the chores and was warming himself by the range.

I can't remember all the relatives that were there, but some stand out in my memory vividly. My brother Earl, cousin Stuart VanVoorhees and Leonard Chapin all about three years old. Mother's brother, Ross, then unmarried was there; cousin Capitola Fassett and daughter Beulah and son, Hartwell. Beulah was a violinist of some note and a very interesting person to me.

Christmas at Grandpa and Grandma Chapin's

The house was decorated with homemade things, including paper bells that folded flat for storage, strings of popcorn and decorated candles. The air was filled with things cooking -- mostly things grown on the Chapin farm; turkey, baked potatoes, boston baked beans with cane molasses, baked apples, pumpkin pie, dried apple pie, dried peach pie, mince meat pie made with pure maple syrup, molasses cake and cookies along with all the dairy products, butter, cottage cheese and cheese.

We had arisen early and by the middle of the forenoon, I was hungry. Grandmas are observing individuals and she herded all the children in the pantry off the kitchen and gave us some molasses cookies. Each of us got just two because grandma said, "You mustn't spoil your dinner."

I'll never forget the smell of grandma's pantry. The aroma of many spices, herbs, dried fruit and molasses that loaded the air with a fragrance that excited my olfactory nerves. The wooden molasses barrel, filled once a year from the sugar cane Grandpa raised and took to the sorghum mill, was in the corner capped with a heavy tight wooden cover and a dipper with a hook on the end of the handle that hung from the side of the barrel. The sides of the large pantry were covered with well supported shelves made of wide whitewood boards and made to store dried and canned fruit and vegetables. There was another barrel for salt pork and a place to hang smoked hams and dried beef. A chopping block with cleavers and butcher knives held a prominent place with space around it for cutting meat.

Dad and Grandpa Chapin came in from the barn and I remember a little about their conversation about the horses. Grandpa marveled at the short time it took to make the trip under the adverse weather conditions. He thought dad had a great pair

Chapter 9

of trotting horses but remarked he would be better off to have heavier draft horses for the farm work. Dad was worried about Theron's exposure to the cold and went over close to him to talk. His concern was well founded. Theron had thawed out and his ears had been frozen and lopped down like a pair of basset hound's ears. Grandma had already applied cold water and some home remedies to lessen the discomfort, but Theron wasn't feeling well and he ended up having trouble with his ears all that winter.

Grandpa had opened up the living room, the parlor, and two downstairs bedrooms and built a wood fire in the parlor stove -- the kind that had mica windows on the sides and in the door so the burning embers glowed through the many little windows. It was a beautiful sight at night when the kerosene lamps were turned low and you sat in near darkness watching the lights reflecting from the burning stove on the room walls. We kids went in the parlor, played games and watched the fire. The big dining room was a busy place, everyone finding something to do getting the food on the table. It was soon ready and as we emerged from the parlor I saw a big, big table filled with food and a row of chairs all around it with grandpa's big swivel chair at one end and grandma's arm chair at the other end. The women had planned where everyone would sit, so we were soon at the table with no fuss. Eating was done together as a family, somewhat formal but, as I remember it, an extremely enjoyable experience. Grandma said grace. I don't remember what grandma included in her conversation with God on that Christmas, but Grandpa and Grandma Chapin, like many Americans of their generation, were deeply religious. They had endured much hardship, had lived through the Civil War, which helped them to appreciate what they had. They loved their country and thanked God every day for their blessings. Christmas wasn't commercialized as it is now. The great emphasis was on the celebration of Christ's birthday -- to them the one who had given the most toward peace, good will and guideposts for the perfect life.

Grandpa carved the turkey and that took a bit of time as he asked everyone if they had a preference. The kids, with limited knowledge of turkey anatomy, took what was served and were glad to get it. Talk and laughter filled the room until we reached a point where the consumption of food had filled us to capacity. Grandma had never heard of child psychology, but she had learned more about how kids think and behave than most people know. She sensed that we were itching to get to doing things and got the attention of everyone at the table, then formally excused us to go and play. We hurried into the parlor and started getting acquainted and speculating on when they might bring out the gifts and exchange presents.

From time to time I glanced in the kitchen and saw the men bring in wood for the stoves and water to be put in the range reservoir for warm water for the dishes and greasy pans. Grandma made all her own soap, molded into large bars and shaved off into hot water for washing dishes. As the dishwater would get too much grease in it from the pots and pans, Grandma would empty it into pails to be carried out as there was no outside drain or sink to empty it in. Soon dishes were done and the food stored in a cold room next to an outside wall.

The adults sauntered into the parlor and I overheard Grandma say, "We can get the gifts now before the men have to leave to go home and feed the stock and milk the cows." I knew there were chores to do and we would have to go home and I was feeling blue over the thoughts of leaving, knowing my cousins would be staying a number of days. Then mother whispered to me, "Your father and Uncle Ed are going home to do the chores and coming back for us tomorrow." I leaped for joy! By then the women were bringing some Christmas things out of hiding and placing them on a table in the corner of the parlor.

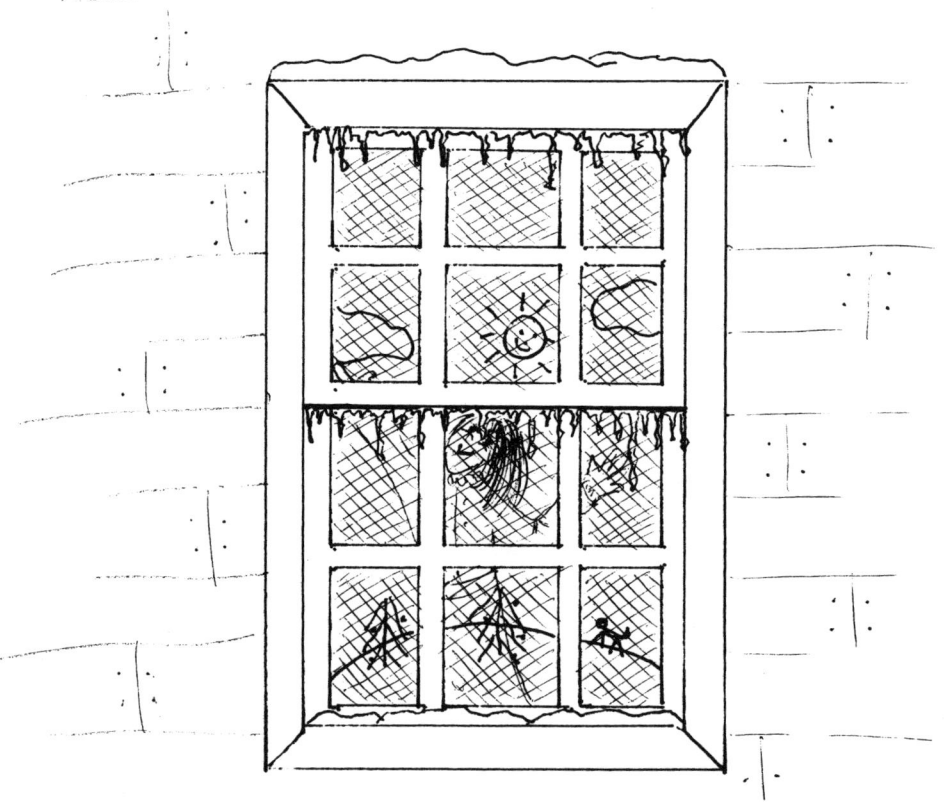

The parlor windows were high. The low temperature on the outside and high humidity on the inside had covered them with a heavy coat of frost. Someone started to etch scenes on the frosted surface and soon most of the adults were in the act.

Chapter 9

I remember how interested I was in the process at the same time impatiently waiting for everyone to get back and get started opening presents. I wasn't in on the planning so I was oblivious to all that was taking place. Sleighbells were heard above the wintry winds and they seemed to be turning in the drive. In a moment they were by the kitchen door and we all rushed to see Santa with his sleigh. Grandpa tied Santa's horses to the hitching post and Santa stumbled in with his pack and dumped the contents on the parlor floor and ran back to his sleigh and slid away in his cutter waving and shouting "Merry Christmas" to all. I am sure it was the real Santa as I have never heard differently.

We opened our gifts. I remember little what anyone got except that they were practical always, including new mittens, stockings, and the like.

It was soon dark and time for bed. I don't remember where the adults slept. It was a big house, but there were a lot of people to bed down. We kids slept on makeshift beds on the parlor floor. Grandpa had a big pile of wood laid neatly beside the heating stove to feed the fire and keep us warm throughout the night. Our mothers tucked us all in, heard our prayers and kissed us goodnight. The kerosene lights were blown out and the light of the moon through the frosted windows gave us light enough to get around. Grandma placed two big pots, one in each bedroom off the parlor, one for boys and one for girls, so we wouldn't have to get out in near zero weather to go to the backhouse. We all did make a trip out there before we undressed for bed, however. I recall having some difficulty getting that part of my anatomy through all those winter clothes by the dim lantern light without getting wet.

It had been an exciting day. We had poured a lot of adrenalin in our blood stream that hadn't had time to work off. We didn't go to sleep, but laughed and horsed around (which is par for kids) and were told repeatedly by different adults to quiet down. The first contacts were gentle suggestions, then more severe directives that later turned into threats. It was then my Great Aunt Capitola Fassett said to her daughter, "Beulah, go in and play for them." Beulah was an accomplished musician and played for Redpath Cautauqua* a number of seasons. I had never heard Beulah play the violin. In fact, I had never heard anyone play the violin who had mastered it. When Beulah started to play, I thought I must be dreaming.

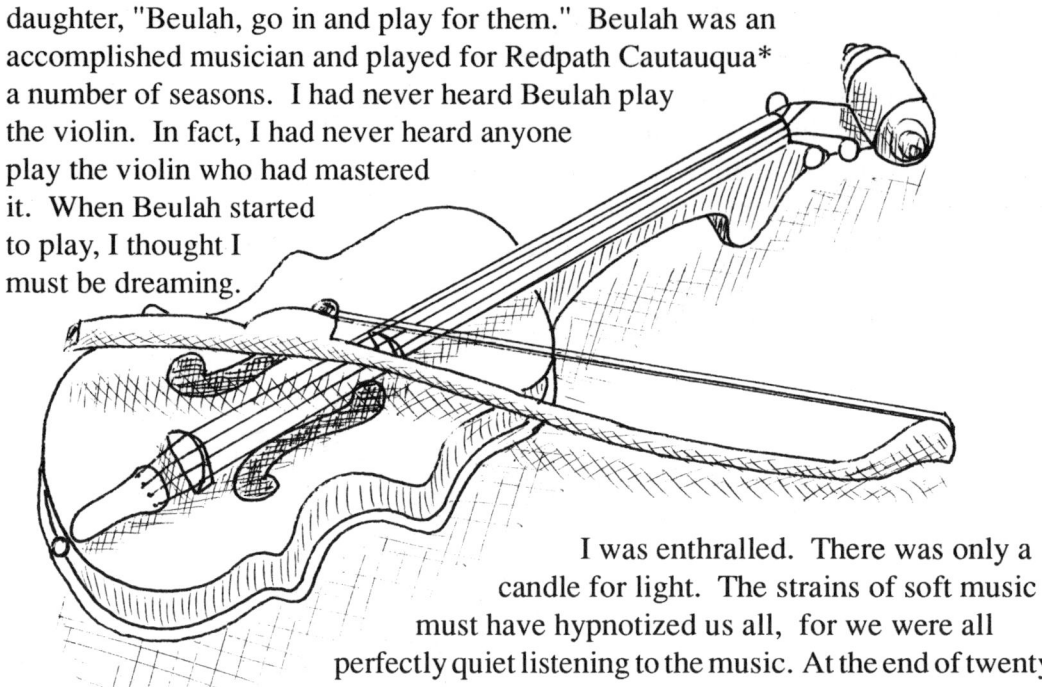

I was enthralled. There was only a candle for light. The strains of soft music must have hypnotized us all, for we were all perfectly quiet listening to the music. At the end of twenty minutes, Beulah stopped playing and started to talk. It was the beginning of a story that unfolded as a mystery and ended on an extremely scary note. My head was covered with the bed sheet and I dared not look out and I suspect every kid in the room was in the same boat because there was not another noise all night. Then Beulah blew out the candle and left.

I awoke with my nostrils filled with the aroma of coffee, bacon and frying ham. The stove was aglow and the whole downstairs warm. My cousins were mostly girls, so I had to dress in the upstairs bedroom my mother slept in to give the girls the warm place by the parlor stove.

We had to wait for Grandpa, Uncle Leonard and Ross to come in from doing the chores as it was a Chapin tradition that the family eat together. It was a fun breakfast; Grandpa and Grandma seemed to have fun joking and laughing with everyone.

---

*The Redpath Chautauquas were traveling groups that operated in the Unied States from 1903 to 1930. They moved from town to town giving a program of lectures, concerts, and recitals in a large tent. These traveling groups brought shows of mixed quality to the people of rural areas. Their popularity decreased with the invention of radio and the development of other forms of entertainment.

Chapter 9

  Dad drove in about the middle of the morning, put Maud and Trilby in the barn and fed them.

  At three in the afternoon we were saying good-bye to our relatives as dad drove the sleigh up by the hitching post by the back door and we crawled in the sleigh under the canvas that covered the stock rack and snuggled up together under the blankets heated by the soapstones that dad had put there earlier. Our trip home was uneventful as dad sat high above us protected by his buffalo coat and heavy blankets driving a team of horses born to run. As we arrived home, settled down and later went to bed, my thoughts returned to the events of the last two days. The thought came to me that we might be doing it again a year from now. Now my thoughts go back seventy-five years with the wish I might do it again, but content with the thought that I've had a great heritage.

Chapter 10

THE BUILDING OF THE BACKHOUSE

It was a real Chick Sales. It had a door on the south and it was a three-holer. If someone wanted to use the outhouse, they would just walk right in (not knowing it was occupied). Upon getting inside, they would feel embarrassed for being there and think, "Why did I act so hastily?" On cold winter days you waited until there was no more time. When you rushed out from the house all bundled up and got inside, you were welcomed by a number of old Sears Roebuck catalogues. During cold weather it was easy to get engrossed in old catalogues.

We had a lot of company and often when one wanted to use the outhouse somebody would barge in on them unknowingly. I decided it should be corrected. My idea was to use a pole quite a bit higher than the backhouse that would raise an arm when someone was inside. I spent many nights thinking how I could design a floor so that an individual's weight on it would point the arm in an upright position. I got the idea to paint the top portion red so it would show up better. I didn't have steel cables, so I would have to use rope instead. Another concept I had was to saw the floor around the three sides and put strap hinges on the door side and fasten ropes to the floor so that a person's weight would cause the arm to go up and indicate it was occupied.

I got involved in so many things, especially on the farm, that I never got to finish my great invention. I thought it was a good idea but I never completed it.

The Building of the Backhouse

So many things happened, it is hard to remember some of them. One thing I remember clearly. Dr. Haynes, our family Doctor, was a strong believer in enemas -- and I remember one especially well.

Earl, for some reason, thought he needed an enema (or more likely he wanted to try out the device he saw hanging in the backhouse). There was a good sized galvanized bucket hanging on the wall with a rubber tube to carry the water down to a plastic end to be inserted. There was a clamp that pinched the tube to turn the water off and on. The bucket was hung high on the wall to increase the water pressure.

Earl was about four years old when he did his little act. He filled the bucket all by himself and got everything in order and tried to give himself an enema. Mother started looking for Earl and found him in the outhouse. He had water everywhere -- on the seats, on the walls and floor. Earl had no explanation except that he needed an enema.

Chapter 11

UNCLE LEONARD

Uncle Leonard was my mother's uncle. He was very fond of chickens and he named them. They usually liked to stay close to the chicken house, but would follow him around the other farm buildings.

One time I was helping Uncle Leonard grind cycle knives. It was a very particular job as the knives had to be held at a certain angle and they were heavy and long.

There was a rod directly above the stone with a tin can fasted to it. The can had a small hole punched in it so that water would drip on the stone and keep the metal cool as you ground.

There were chickens everywhere and often one would hop on the stone while it was turning and take a walk on the top of it. I waited until a big Plymouth Rock rooster mounted the wheel and I reached up and pulled out some of his tail feathers. Uncle Leonard stopped the grindstone and said, "That's a cruel thing to do." He pulled my hair and asked, "How do you like it?" I felt real bad. I thought to myself, "I'll never treat a chicken like that again."

Chapter 12

A TRAIN RIDE FROM ALBION

    The things I learned from my brother, Lynn, and the toy steam engine we had helped me to better understand locomotives. As the engineer pulled out of Albion, he slowly opened the throttle. I felt the train move, then surge ahead in increasing rhythmic succession as each piston reached its greatest leverage on the drive rods. Hot cinders blown from the exhaust through the smoke stack came through the coach windows. The engine's exhaust soon came in quick succession and the click-click sound of the wheels on the rail joints registered a healthy speed.

    Passengers talking above the train noise brought about a festive atmosphere. Everyone seemed to be in a good mood. The engineer blew the whistle at all road crossings and it could be heard inside the coach above the din of the many voices. The blue uniformed conductor appeared in our coach door and punched our tickets and talked to some of the passengers. When it started to get dark, the conductor turned on the lights, which enhanced the interior of the train cars.

    Suddenly the locomotive's exhaust couldn't be heard and I sensed we were coasting into Homer, twenty minutes after we left Albion. The application of the air brakes sent a low thundering noise throughout the train as we came to a stop.

    I left the train and walked into the darkness looking for my father. I could see the depot lights and the brakeman with his red, white and blue lantern. I could also see lanterns on the buggies by the hitching posts. I found dad in front of the depot waiting for me. The rat-a-tat-tat of the telegraph caught my ear as I walked past the depot to where dad stood.

A Train Ride From Albion

As we neared the buggy with the aid of the kerosene lantern hanging high on the dashboard, I noticed dad had driven our horses, Maud and Trilby. I took time to pat each one on the nose before we left.

Dad got in the buggy while I untied the lines to the bridles, buckled them into the harness, got in the buggy and we rode off into the night.

It was a sweeping change from the train to an open buggy. Those great trotting horses took us home two and a half miles at a fast pace. We talked about my experience and the day's happenings as we rode along in the buggy. Home and in bed, as I dropped to sleep, I thought of the two or three weeks it would be before I would get the results of the county eighth grade tests I had taken in Albion that day.

The next morning I awoke with an unburdened feeling as school was behind me for the summer. During the spring I worked the daylight hours planting and it was to my liking. I was soon in the field behind the Oliver walking plow turning over the sod and watching the birds pluck angle worms from the furrows.

The anticipation of the five acres dad gave me each year to work for my own profit, the swimming hole, fishing on the St. Joe and activities at Cook's Prairie Church quickened my step. It was going to be a great summer.

Chapter 13

WHEN EARL GOT CUT WITH AN AXE

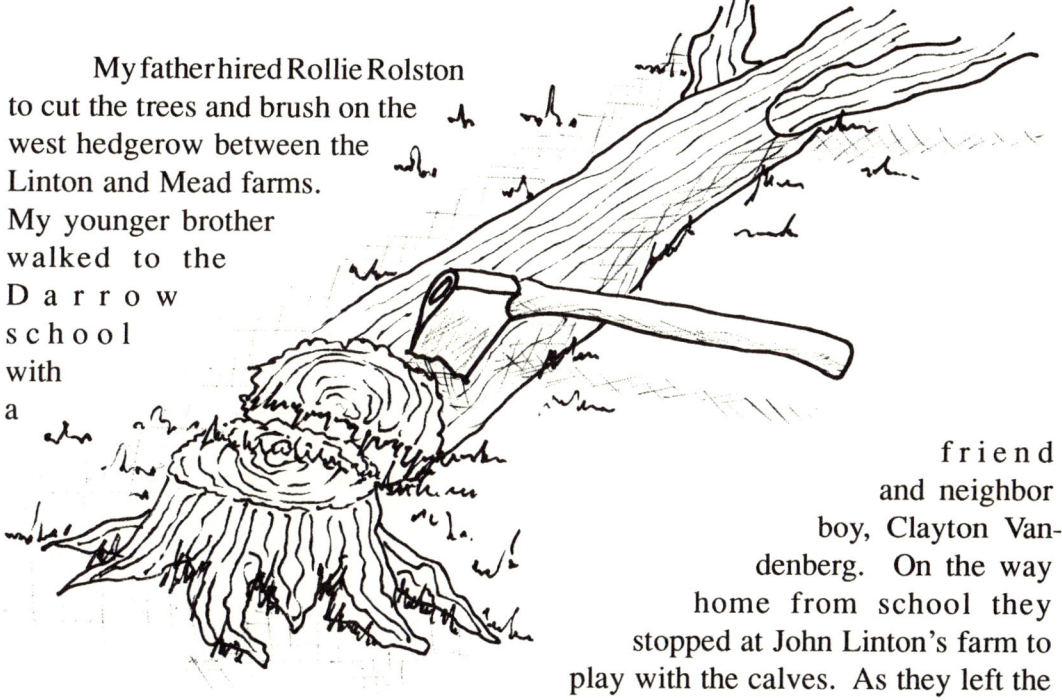

My father hired Rollie Rolston to cut the trees and brush on the west hedgerow between the Linton and Mead farms. My younger brother walked to the Darrow school with a friend and neighbor boy, Clayton Vandenberg. On the way home from school they stopped at John Linton's farm to play with the calves. As they left the Linton barn and neared the hedgerow, Rollie fell a big tree so they went over to the hedgerow to enjoy the excitement. The tree, a pignut hickory*, lay on the ground with its limbs extending from the trunk in many directions making it an interesting test to a boy's climbing skills.

It was before the invention of the chain saw. All cutting had to be done with an axe, a one man saw or a buck saw. If there were two men a two-man saw could be used. As Rollie finished cutting off the top limbs of the tree the boys ended their climbing and straddled the big log. Then Rollie wanted to plant his axe in the big hickory log. He swung his axe hard over his shoulder and close to Earl on the log. As he did so, Earl swung his leg over the other side of the log to avoid being hit with the axe, but was struck on top of the instep. It cut through his overshoe, shoe and into his foot. Rollie grabbed Earl and carried him to the house all the time hanging on to the foot to help keep it from bleeding. Mother looked out the window and spotted

When Earl Got Cut with an Axe

Rollie carrying Earl and met him at the door. He was exhausted after carrying Earl a half mile across the fields. Mother nervously asked, "What happened?" Rollie said, as he breathed heavily, "I cut Earl's foot with an axe." Immediately mother stepped to the phone and called Dr. Haynes and he came right out to the house. My father came in the house about the time the doctor arrived and soon got the story of what happened.

The doctor approached Earl lying on the bed with his winter clothes on and assured him that he would take good care of him (and got a big smile in return). Before he went further, he removed Earl's shoe and stocking and asked him to move his toes -- he could move each of them so he knew no cords were cut and he wouldn't be lame.

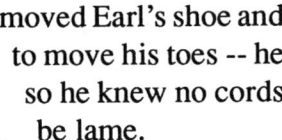

He then opened up his case and took out a mask and a bottle of chloroform and told my father how to use it. He poured a little chloroform on the pad and held it over Earl's nose and asked him to take a deep breath. A few more shots of chloroform and Earl was completely out. Then, with mother's help, the doctor removed Earl's coat.

The doctor looked at Earl and decided he needed more chloroform so he said to Dad, "Pour a little more on the pad." He cleaned the cut with soap and water and later with antiseptic, then looked through his case for the right needle and catgut to sew up the wound. It took fourteen stitches.

My father put up a cot in their upstairs bedroom so mother could watch Earl until he was well. Later that afternoon I rushed home from high school and bounced into the house and instantly smelled chloroform. I imagined many things in lightening succession that might have happened before I found mother to tell me what took place. She said that Earl had been cut on the foot with an axe and explained all the things that had happened that afternoon and attempted to put my mind at rest. I went in the see Earl but he was still groggy from the chloroform. As I went about my chores, I missed him being in the barn with me and worried about his being able to walk normally again.

In a few weeks he was back in school and perfectly normal again, but he always carried a big scar on his foot where he was cut with an axe.

---

*A pignut is a "wild" hickory nut tree. Pigs liked to eat the hard nuts that fell on the ground and they made a loud crunch when they chewed them. We didn't eat the nuts because they were so bitter.

Chapter 14

MY FIRST STATIONARY GASOLINE ENGINE

Either through my exposure to farm machinery or simply by nature, I was fascinated with anything of a mechanical nature early in my childhood. This profound interest in machines got me into the stationary gasoline engine room at the Clarendon grain elevator where I went with my father to sell our wheat.

The grain elevator was a tall building on the Michigan Central Railroad. The elevator was owned and operated by a close friend of my father's, John Ballentine. When we would go there with a team of horses pulling a lumber wagon loaded with canvas bags filled with wheat, John, knowing my interest in engines would take me by the hand to the engine room. The engines had two thirty-inch flywheels. The engine took up much of the space where it was housed under the elevator. John would seat me on a plank bench near the engine explaining what might happen if I got off the bench and got caught in the engine flywheels. I never budged from the bench and often sat there over an hour at a time watching the engine run while dad unloaded the wheat.

Starting the engine was a tense, exciting moment for me. John always followed the same procedure, opening the petcock on the cylinder head, filling it with gasoline from an oil can used for that purpose, and turning the flywheels to draw the charge into the cylinder. He then turned the flywheels so the crankshaft was past dead center, closed the petcock, then closed a knife switch wired to drycell batteries for the ignition. The engine started with a thunderous explosion that brought my hands over my ears to muffle the sound. When the engine got up to speed, the governor took

My First Stationary Gasoline Engine

over. John then moved a long lever shifting the belt from the idler pulley to the pulley on the line shaft. This transmitted the power to the endless belt with buckets fastened to it carrying the grain to the top of the elevator where it could be directed into separate bins by pipes. Before John left the engine room he motioned to me, above the engine noise, to stay on the bench and left to tend the elevator.

Some years later John sent word that he wanted me to come down to the store. The Ballentine brothers, John and Lew, ran a General Store in Clarendon. Arriving at the store, John presented me with an electric engine, a replica of the two-flywheel gasoline engine. It was mounted on a nice box that contained two telephone batteries for power. I lost track of the engine years ago, but I'll always cherish the memory of that gift.

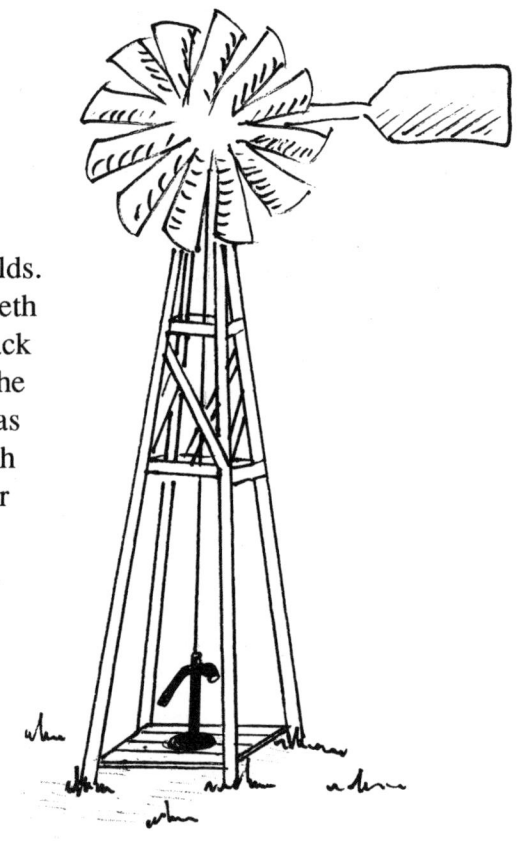

Windmills dotted the countryside in Southern Michigan when I was a boy. They were great labor saving machines to pump water for the stock. Windless days found us back on the pump handle keeping ahead of a herd of thirsty cattle. The pumping often fell to the boys and girls on the farm as the men were working in the fields.

During the beginning of the twentieth century, the gasoline engine and pump jack came on the market. The jack was bolted to the pump and the engine to the floor. Power was transmitted from the engine to the jack with a flat belt. This made cheap power for pumping independent of the wind.

T. J. Smith, who lived down the road a piece from us, decided he'd had enough of windmills and bought an engine and jack. About a month later I was at Mr. Smith's house and saw the new engine and asked him how he liked it. The descriptive adjectives he used to describe it were extremely uncomplimentary. He hadn't lived in the gasoline engine age and had never been able to start it. I said, "Would you sell it?" "I'd sell the whole kit and caboodle for twenty dollars!" I had ten dollars, so I said, "I'll run home quick and talk with

Chapter 14

my mother." I rode my bicycle down that road spitting gravel off my back wheel all the way. I rode in the yard, found my mother and between heavy breathing told her about my good deal.

"It's a new, 2 1/2 horsepower, and has a Webster magneto. We could have power to run things on the farm and all you would have to do is loan me ten dollars." I must have convinced mother I'd found a bargain, for she said, "Go ahead

and buy it." I was back at the Smith farm with the twenty dollars in a short time.

The next day I drove over to the Smith farm to get my engine. Mr. Smith helped me unbolt the engine from the wellhouse floor and the pump jack from the pump and, with the use of skids and muscle power, the two of us loaded it on the wagon.

As I drove the team and wagon out of the drive I turned and waved to Mr. Smith standing by the wellhouse under his windmill. As he waved his arm in return I sensed we were both happy with our deal, he getting rid of an engine he couldn't start and I with a source of power I could put to use. As I drove on I thought of Mr. Smith as a successful farmer about to retire, who grew up in the horse and buggy days, now finding it impossible to operate a gasoline engine to pump his water. For the first time in my life I had the thought that we might be entering a new period in farming where we might be using gasoline powered engines in place of horses as a source of farm power.

As I entered the road my eyes centered on the engine on the floor of the wagon. I wrapped the lines around the front stantion of the wagon rack and let the team take a leisurely gait home. My profound interest in my new engine made me oblivious of my surroundings. Having been kept in the wellhouse protected from the weather, its green paint, cylinder oil drip and brass grease cups shone brightly in the mid-day sun. I noticed the well preserved paint on the dark green cast iron flywheels and water jacket. I whistled with delight as I rediscovered the magneto making it possible to run it without batteries. The horses quickened their step, indicating we were near home. As I turned in our driveway, the heavy wagon wheels rolling over the gravel stones alerted Ma, who came dashing out of the house wiping her wet hands on her apron. "Let me get a good look!" she said as I came to a stop where she could peer over the side of the wagon. "It looks like new," she said as I jumped off the wagon

My First Stationary Gasoline Engine

and replied, "It's as good as new. I'm going to leave the wagon here and put the team in the barn so we can run the engine on the wagon when dad gets here." I scurried around and unhooked the tugs from the whippletrees and fastened them to the hooks on the hip straps. This gave enough clearance so I could slip the yoke off the wagon tongue and unbuckle it and drop it to the ground. The horses freed, walked to the stock tank for a drink while I finished unfastening the harnesses ready to slip them off when the horses went in their stalls. While the horses finished drinking, I ran in the barn ahead of them, removed the heavy harness and hung them on wooden pegs as they entered the stall, then put a pan of oats in each feed box.

Dad soon came home from town with the horse and buggy. While he was unhitching his horse and letting it in the barn, I talked to him barely stopping to take a breath, enraptured with my engine deal. My dad was short on being demonstrative but a good listener. As we approached the wagon, he saw it and appeared to be pleased with its appearance. "Does it run?" he kiddingly asked, whereby I jumped on the wagon, grabbed the heavy cast iron crank and slipped it on the crankshaft next to the flywheel. I rocked the flywheel as I choked it so the piston would draw gasoline in the cylinder. Then I cranked it and the second time over it started. It took only seconds to gain speed, then the governor kept it that way. My mother, dad, brother Earl, and I sat on the wagon rack and watched it run for a spell while we talked about how we could use it. Two things were mentioned that seemed practical; a buzz saw for cutting wood and power to run mother's hand cranked washing machine.

The next day dad ordered a buzz saw from an ad in the Popular Mechanics Magazine. It was made in Milwaukee and three weeks later it came by freight and Dad and I picked it up at the railroad station in Homer. It being summer, I worked fervently on a platform for the engine and saw. I found two hardwood timbers 4" x 4" and tapered them with an axe on one end so they could be pulled over rough ground. I nailed a plank over the top, making a platform about 3' x 8' long. I drilled holes in the tapered ends of the 4" x 4" timbers to accommodate a log chain so it could be pulled by my horse, Nancy. I bolted the engine and the buzz saw the right distance apart so the belt would be tight. I had to cross the belt to make the saw turn the right

Chapter 14

direction, which was good, for it gave more contact with the surface on each pulley. When I got it finished I harnessed my horse Nancy to pull it over to the woodpile to try it out. I decided to put Nancy back in the barn because she had never heard an engine run and might run away.

I was nervous when I started the rig, as I had no experience running a buzz saw. I started it and moved cautiously as I watched it run. After it had run a short time, I decided to cut some wood. I had on canvas gloves to protect my hands, which I soon learned was a poor thing to do. My second cut had a bend in the wood that caused it to turn as it caught the saw and threw my hand onto the saw. Instantly all that was left of my glove was its palm, the rest was in shreds. I was fortunate, for it only scratched my hand. It 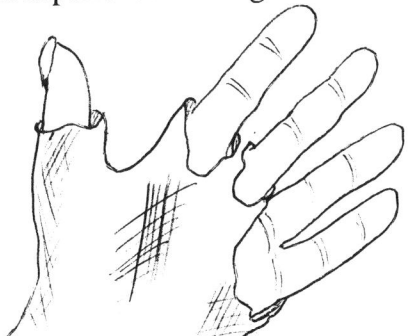 could have cut my hand off. I soon learned a lot about using a saw attached to power.

Wire fences were rapidly replacing old rail fences. Farmers would put up wire fences and I would get a lot of jobs hitching my horse Nancy on the buzz saw and go up the fence row sawing the rails as I went. I spent many Saturdays doing this.

Then there was my mother's washing machine. It had a round wooden tub held together with steel bands. The washer was elevated off the floor by four wooden legs. It was a hand propelled machine. It had a wooden handle about eighteen inches long that the operator moved back and forth propelling the cast iron mechanism that washed the clothes. This machine had a cast iron flywheel about eighteen inches in diameter and one and one half inches wide, that made it easier to keep it at a constant speed. The whole mechanism was fastened to a hinged cover that could be opened to put in the clothes.

I made a skid similar to the one for the buzz saw on which to mount the engine and washer. The belt that came with the engine was six inches wide and had to be lined up perfectly to keep it on the washing machine flywheel. It took the better part of two days making my skid and mounting the engine and washer. When I got it together, I turned it quite a few times by hand to make sure it stayed on the washing machine flywheel. The washer was back of the house on the grass and mother was concerned that her washing would get dirty before she got it hung up.

Our well water was hard, so we used rain water that ran off our house into eaves that in turn ran into our cistern. Our cistern was made of concrete, round, in the ground, and about ten feet deep. A cistern pitcher pump was used to fill pails to be carried into the kitchen and heated on the range. This day mother and I carried the hot water out and put it in the washer, then added shaved Fels Naptha soap.

My First Stationary Gasoline Engine

I was nervous experimenting with a strange contraption, especially when it included mother's washing machine. We finally had everything set ready to go. Mother was game for anything, but I imagine she was tied up in knots, as I headed for the engine to start it. It started instantly and the washing machine had never run that fast. Mother and I were happy and pleased as we watched it run seemingly effortless. I ran across the road to get dad, who was cultivating corn. As he approached the engine running the machine he had a smile on his face. As we all sat on the back steps, we saw soap suds come from around the cover and run over the sides and on the ground. Dad warned, "You better slow that engine down a bit. It will wear out the washer." Whereby I stepped up and adjusted the governor so the engine would run slower. When I slowed it down the wide belt slipped, unnoticed, inside the flywheel on the washer and then caught in the flywheel of the engine. Instantly all heck broke loose. The momentum of the engine flywheels tore the washer from the skid, lifted it about four feet in the air and bashed it on the ground in many pieces.

Mother's washing was in the mud and she was crying. Dad walked back across the road without comment to resume his cultivating. I felt as if I had been hit by a bolt of lightning. Mother gathered up her clothes and started washing them out by hand in the kitchen. After the initial shock, I started looking things over and couldn't find any pieces broken. I started putting it back together, fitting the staves in place and driving the metal bands back on the butt (like a barrel). By night I had it all back together, but this time I made guides to keep the belt on the washing machine flywheel.

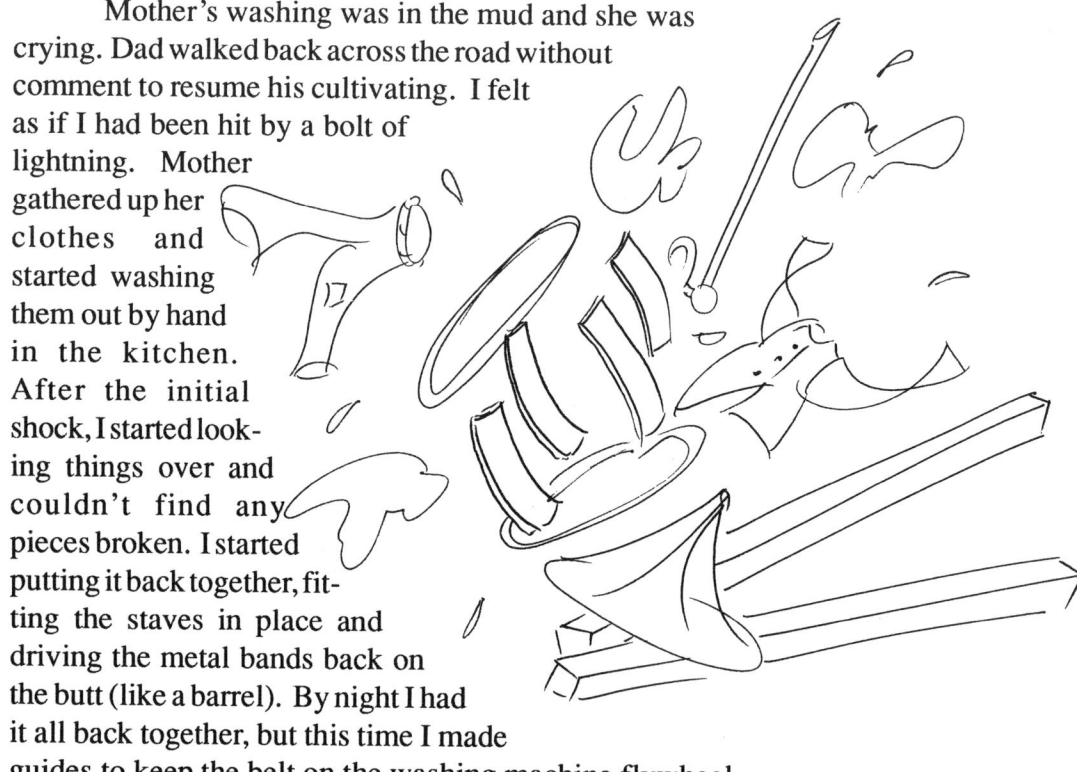

We continued to use the machine all that next summer, but it gradually wore out the washing machine.

Chapter 15

THE CLARENDON STORE FIRE

The Clarendon store was about one mile from the farm house where we lived. The New York Central Railroad came through Clarendon and the trains often stopped to let off and pick up passengers. Lew Ballentine, one of the brothers who owned the General Store was also the ticket agent. He had an office behind one of the counters where he sold tickets to people going to different places around the country. Clarendon was the center of a farming community. The railroad was a busy place with about twenty trains going through each day. Most were freight trains pulling cars loaded with lime to be used in the making of cement at a cement factory. I was told the plant was in Jackson, Michigan, about 30 miles from Clarendon.

South of the store about a mile was a water tower to furnish the steam locomotives with water. This tower was probably forty feet high. These engines were steam powered -- water was heated in a boiler by coal which produced the steam. Most of the trains would stop to refill their water supply there. They would fill the 'tender' from the overhead tank.

I heard my father call "FIRE!" about three o'clock in the morning. We had a wall phone downstairs so I believe my father had been up before to answer the "fire call" on the phone. Whenever a rural fire was reported, the telephone operator would give long intermittent rings on the lines and then give the location of the fire. Everyone who could would immediately hurry to the fire to give assistance. It woke me up and I was up ready to accompany my father to the fire. My father had already started dressing.

My mother didn't agree about my going. She thought I would get too cold (besides the danger I would encounter). My father thought differently. He thought I should go -- which I did! We hooked the horse on the buggy and drove away in the dark.

The first thing the Ballentine brothers, owners of the store, did was to give everyone who came to help a brand new pair of overalls to work in. We put them on and wore them. It was a general store to accommodate all the necessities of the surrounding community, including a stock of shot gun shells. When that area got too hot, they began to explode. They were in the back of the store. There was lots of noise,

but no one got hit. A short time later the fire reached the canned beans and those exploded spreading beans all over. Between the two we had a lot of popping going on.

The store finally burned down, only the four cement walls were left. In spite of all odds, they built a new store right where the other one stood. They had good weather so it didn't take them long. We had a new store in the spring where the men could again gather on the front porch to sit and discuss the weather, the crops, politics and sometimes play checkers.

Chapter 16

THE INVITATION

Things were going at an even keel with our two cousins who spent every summer on our farm. As soon as school was out, they were already packed for the old homestead. Stuart lived in North Tonawanda, New York State, and Leonard was from Battle Creek (about thirty miles from our farm). I was older than any of the boys, about six or seven years their senior. Being older, I had quite a bit to say about how they did things while on the farm. This included my younger brother, whom I actually had little control over.

I never really found out who got the idea, but it was to send a postal card to Earl from the Homer post office from Maurine Cilley bearing her signature either copied by Leonard or Stuart. The invitation was to invite Earl to a party she was having at her house. Maurine lived on a farm about two and a half miles east of our farm. This card was fictitious and sent illegally.

The card was delivered by our own rural carrier, Mr. Daniels. When Earl got it, he was pleased to get a card from such a pretty girl. Leonard and Stuart read it with interest and commented on it favorably.

In the meantime, I started thinking about it and wondered what I could find out. I felt sorry for Earl, especially in a situation like he was in. Knowing Earl, I couldn't understand how he could be taken

The Invitation

in on an incident of that nature. After pondering over it for awhile, I planned to go ahead with my investigation. I soon found out that it wasn't an easy task, for it had its ups and downs as the plot got more complicated. I decided I could approach my cousins with the idea that it seemingly was an unfair thing to do because it could border on mail fraud and involve the United States' mail. It also contained a false signature.

As I was putting the pieces of their act together, I had a feeling I should go to the limit with them.

After a few days, I started talking to Stuart and Leonard separately, and spelling out the seriousness of the whole matter. I dwelled on mail fraud and signing of the card as a federal offense. Aunt Matt, Stuart's mother, and my mother, Lillian, went along with my whole warning.

As time passed, Stuart and Leonard started seeing the seriousness of the predicament. It affected Stuart in a religious way. Early one morning he couldn't find his New Testament and asked Aunt Matt for her's. Leonard went around with a pained look on his face and he moved slowly as if he had a lot on his mind.

After a week spent in their misery, Stuart and Leonard finally gave in and told Earl they were sorry for what they had done. It was a victory for Earl because he was able to picture what had taken place. He was relieved in a way, realizing it was all fictitious, he hadn't gone to the party and been embarrassed, and it was all past history.

Chapter 17

CHEWING TOBACCO

We had two doctors in our town and surrounding county. Folks who had Dr. Thompson were positive he could cure you of any disease you might have. Others felt Dr. Haynes was a miracle doctor who couldn't make a mistake. People who had either of these doctors felt a nearness to him; they needed them not only for health but for advice in many things.

Dr. Haynes was our family doctor. He was a short, chubby man who always wore a bow tie, a dark suit with a vest and a pocket watch fastened with a heavy gold chain. He took short steps but never seemed to be hurried even under stressful circumstances. He had a reputation as having an excellent bedside manner. Socially he was a jolly good fellow and could often see the funny side of serious situations. As a boy I respected him as a doctor and liked to be around him.

During epidemics he would drive his horse and buggy by our farm house in all kinds of weather going many hours without sleep. Mother would see him coming down the road often in a heavy snow storm or pouring rain and would call to dad, "Dr. Haynes is driving in." Dad would go out, unhook the horse from the buggy and put it in the barn, rub it down and feed it. Dr. Haynes would come in and lie down on the bedroom off our living room without exchanging a word. Mother would take off his shoes, cover him with a blanket and he would tell her when he wanted to be called.

Chewing Tobacco

My father always gave me a few acres to raise crops of my own. The year I was 14 he let me have seven acres down by the St. Joe River. On a Saturday morning in the middle of April I loaded the Oliver 90 walking plow on the stoneboat and went to the field by the river. A stoneboat is made of hardwood planks, sawed to turn up on one end and used to move stones, stumps and small farm machinery by horse power. It has no runners, its very hard to pull and rough to ride on. Before I could get the horses hooked to the plow I was hailed by some boys from town who arrived on the scene chewing tobacco. They took great delight showing me how accurately they could spit tobacco juice. They offered me some and I took a small pinch. They said, "Come on, take a big cud!" I had never heard of peer pressure up until then, but I was introduced to it right there, so I took a big one.

It was a warm day and the water was quite cool, but we decided to go swimming in our old swimming hole in the St. Joe River. Every time I dove in that cold water I involuntarily swallowed some tobacco juice. After swimming we hurriedly put on our clothes to get warm. I sat on a stump on the river bank to put on my socks and shoes. Upon getting up I fell over on the river bank and was so dizzy I couldn't stand up. I had stomach cramps and felt like I'd been hit by lightning. The boys could see I wasn't going to be able to walk home. They knew little about horses, harnesses, whippletrees and things like that, but they got the team hooked to the stone boat and loaded me on it and drove me to the house. It was the worst half mile ride I've ever had and I lived through it because I was young, strong and tough.

Arriving home, the boys carried me in the house. My mother was distraught thinking I'd had a sun stroke. She quickly stepped to the wall phone, called the operator and asked for Dr. Haynes. He drove out in his two passenger Saxon and came in the bedroom where I was still feeling pretty sick. He opened up his little satchel where he carried his instruments and pills. Mother stood by his side listening for a clue. He said to my mother, "Lillie, go in the kitchen and get a dish to put some pills in." While mother was gone he bent over me and said, "Have you been chewing tobacco?" I shook my head affirmatively and by then mother was back with the dish. Dr. Haynes said to mother that I didn't have sun stroke, that it was just an upset stomach and nothing to worry about. The doctor gave me some pills and I never knew what they were for. It could have been a cure for chewing tobacco because I've never chewed the stuff since that one time.

Chapter 18

DAD'S STEADY CHARACTER

    I started cutting Dad's hair when I was in high school and continued to do it while I was in college. After I was married and lived one hundred and twenty miles away, I would come down to visit and sometimes his hair would get pretty long -- but he always waited.

    The best light for cutting hair was in the dining room by the outside door. Mother had her sewing machine there next to the doorway. The rural telephone was a wooden box-like affair, about 12 x 30 inches, fastened to the wall nearby. It contained the necessary bell that called you to the phone and two dry cell batteries powered it. Many had a shelf attached on which to keep notes.

    One day I was cutting Dad's hair when a storm came up with lots of wind with it. The tumble weeds were blowing across the fields and yard and against the house. Every time they bounced, they would lose some seeds until the seeds were gone (that's the way they propagated).

    The lightning continued and it got darker and darker. I could see lightning across the road in front of the house. Finally, the lightning struck the house and the phone went crashing to the floor. Dad didn't move. All he said was, "That was pretty close." Just an example of his steady nerves and unexcitable nature.

    Where the lightning struck the house, it splintered a trim board. That was still there when the farm was sold 25 years later.

Chapter 19

WHEN PERCY AND I BUILT THE CANNON

It all started as we listened to the old Civil War Veterans tell about loading the cannons and muzzle loading rifles. The muskets used black powder carried in a powder horn to keep it dry. The horn was actually a cow's horn shaved off on both the big and tip ends with a wooden cap to fit the big end and a tight fitting wooden plug for the tip end. They loaded the musket by pouring a small amount of black powder into the muzzle end of the musket followed by a paper wad to hold the powder in and then rammed it with a ram rod that was fastened to the underside of the musket barrel. A lead ball was put in next, followed by another paper wad to keep the ball from falling out. That was rammed in and now it was ready to fire.

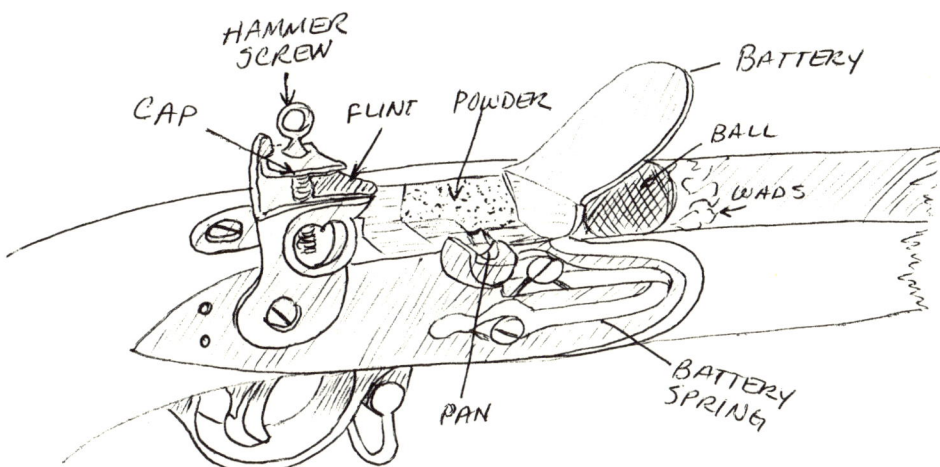

The old veterans had some fascinating stories about the old flintlock muskets, especially when the weather was humid and they refused to fire. The muskets worked on the principle that a piece of steel on the hammer would graze a piece of flint, making a spark as the trigger was pulled, and the gun would go off. Later they invented the cap so when the hammer came down over the cap it ignited the charge.

When Percy and I Built the Cannon

Capt. Garrison played a lot of checkers at the Clarendon Store. Civil War Veterans would often drop in and play with him and spin tall tales about their army life. My Uncle Leonard Chapin and my Uncle Charlie Gardner were in the Civil War together and when they would meet, often at our house, I would sit by the hour and listen to their episodes. From these stories I found out how to load a musket and got the idea of making a cannon.

My close friend, Percy Ballentine, lived in the second house east of us. Percy was a cautious, conservative lad, but when we started talking about building a cannon, he was full of drive to get going on it. We made a lot of quiet inquiries so as not to raise the apprehension of our folks for fear it might backfire.

My father had a good farm workshop for repairing harnesses and farm machinery. We spent a lot of time there rummaging through old farm machinery looking for parts to make a cannon. We had great ideas of what a cannon would do, but were greenhorns when it came to making one. When Percy and I were ransacking through things in our shop one night after school, I ran onto a piece of seamless pipe an inch and half in diameter and eighteen inches long. I said to Percy, "What do you think of this?" He looked it over and came back with the idea that he thought I had found the barrel for the cannon, but was concerned that it was open on both ends. I picked it up and looked it over for a few minutes and Mr. Matson, our Clarendon blacksmith, came to my mind. "He could close one end by welding it in his forge," I told Percy. We wasted no time strapping the pipe on my bicycle, gathering some eggs from the henhouse to pay Mr. Matson and headed for Clarendon. Clarendon had about ten houses, a general store, the Gleaner Hall, a grain elevator and a depot on the Michigan Central Railroad. When we got to the blacksmith shop, Mr. Matson was shoeing a horse and we had to wait until he was through. On finishing his shoeing he looked up and with a Swedish accent asked, "What you boys got today?" We produced the pipe and said we wanted one end welded shut. He used long tongs to put it in the forge and covered it with hot coals and then pumped the bellows on the forge until the end of the pipe was white hot. He then laid it on the edge of the forge and put flux on the part he was going to weld. Grabbing it with the tongs, he laid it on the big anvil and struck it with his heavy maul and it was welded shut.

Watching the cannon barrel taking shape under the blacksmith's hammer, we remembered that cannons needed a fuse and a small hole should be drilled in the closed end of the barrel. As the barrel laid on the forge we approached Mr. Matson about drilling it. He looked straight at us with a puzzled look and said, "What yer making?" We said, "A cannon." He turned to put the cannon barrel in water to cool it, then started to drill it as he commented, "You're goin' to get your heads blowed off."

Chapter 19

With the cannon fuse hole drilled we paid Mr. Matson with eggs, strapped the cannon barrel on my bicycle and took off for home. When we got to my house, it was getting late. Percy had chores to do and he left for home. I put the cannon barrel in the shop and went to the barn to start my chores.

When I came in the barn, Mr. Dolittle was feeding the cows. A few years earlier Anthony Dolittle's wife died and my father and mother had taken him in to live with us. He lived with us until shortly before he died (by that time he had gone to live with his daughter). He was neat, amiable, very pleasant to have around, but was the most deliberate, slowest person I have ever known. It took him about a half hour to dress to go outdoors.

The next day we scurried home from school to get going on the cannon. The barrel solved, we probed the farm shop to find a base to mount it on. We thought it should be heavy for when we fired it we imagined it would kick back with great force and tip it over. We remembered the veterans telling us about the cannons, mounted on wheels, rolling back when they fired them. We finally stumbled on the idea of using dad's chopping block. We hesitated using it for it was used for so many things on the farm (like mending harnesses and chopping off chicken's heads). It was made of apple wood, heavy, tough and almost impossible to split. It seemed like the most suitable object so we decided to use it anyway.

Now we had the problem of mounting the cannon barrel on it. We looked at a lot of things in the shop before we arrived at the idea of holding it on the chopping block with two pieces of strap iron with lag screws on each side.

We found two pieces of strap iron, hammered them to fit the curvature of the barrel and started drilling the holes for the lag screws. My father had a brace and some drills. We took turns drilling but seemed to be making little progress. I started drilling and said, "Percy, climb on my back so I can get more pressure on the drill." Exerting so much pressure on the brace with Percy on my back made it hard for me to breathe. We took turns drilling and in about two hours had the four holes through the strap iron and into the block. We placed the barrel on the block, laid the two pieces of strap iron over the barrel in line with the holes. We tightened the lag screws with long wrenches to get more leverage. The whole contraption was about two feet high, ungainly, heavy and, of course, hard to move. All it lacked was some gun powder and a fuse to get it ready to shoot.

We waited for days for a convenient time to fire it. It wasn't until the Calhoun County Fair time in Marshall that Dad said, before I went to school, that he and mother would be going to the fair and would be taking Earl with them. I was to start the chores as they might be late getting home. On the way to school I talked to Percy.

When Percy and I Built the Cannon

"Today would be a good day to fire the cannon." With my folks gone, he thought so, too. It was a long day at school with the cannon shooting on our minds.

School out for the day, we stampeded home like a crow flies, vaulting fences -- anything to make time. Entering our farm shop out of breath but happy that we had about reached our goal. We pulled and tugged, exhausted and out of breath as we dragged the cannon back of the shop and pointed it toward some hickory trees where cows were pastured. We needed a fuse and some powder. My father had two old powder horns filled with black powder that he kept upstairs in our house. They had caked solid. We hammered them against the floor to get the powder loose and poured it into an old coffee mug until it was full. Firecrackers from the fourth of July provided us with some fuses. We decided to use two tied together to make them longer.

We put the fuse in the small hole Mr. Matson had drilled in the butt of the cannon so it would be in contact with the powder. We turned the barrel pointing up and poured in a portion of the powder. There was some discussion as to the amount of gun powder to use. The final decision was to use all the powder for it was old and might have lost some of its power. We poured the rest of it in and rammed it with a long rod with the help of a ball pean hammer. We then inserted a paper wad and rammed that in, too. By this time it was getting late and we became excited and jittery. In our rush we finally realized we didn't have shot so we substituted washers, wood screws, nails and other small objects we found in the shop. We put them in the cannon barrel, rammed them home and packed them in with another paper wad. We were surprised to find the barrel two thirds full of powder, shot and wads.

West of the shop we had a big barn, then a gate, a windmill, a watering tank for the stock and the shop. A high board fence, with boards running vertically, making it difficult to scale, ran from the shop to a corncrib then turned right angles to the North for about thirty feet to our buggy shed. We had the cannon behind the shop aimed North and were ready to fire it.

The pressure was great to ignite the cannon before the folks got home from the fair. We had to decide who was going to light the fuse. Percy suggested we draw cuts and I agreed that was fair. We put straws in a paper sack and decided the one who got the shortest one won the distinction of lighting the cannon. I think neither of us wanted it for when the chips were down there were hazards and a real chance of being hurt. We each reluctantly reached in the sack and drew out a straw and Percy danced

Chapter 19

around as he exclaimed, "You, Stephen, got the short one!" In my effort to lose no time, it did enter my mind the cannon was pointed toward some cattle in the pasture. Somebody besides Percy seemed to be present and whispering in my ear, "Don't take chances," and "Be cautious." I did take quite a while to figure out how I was going to climb the fence after I lit the fuse. The fence was taller than I was for I was only fifteen years old and the boards ran up and down making it hard to scale. I tried different ways to climb it and discovered by putting my hands on top of the fence and swinging my legs over the top and falling on the other side, was the quickest way to get over.

The cannon was about ten feet from the fence. I practiced going over the fence a number of times before I actually fired it. Measuring my stride and digging holes in the ground to get a firmer toe-hold worked out so I had it down pat. Percy was peeking through a knothole in the fence as I finally took the wooden matches from my pocket and lit the fuse. As soon as the fuse started to sputter I beat it for the fence, scaled it and fell on the other side. Percy and I ran up by the house to wait for the

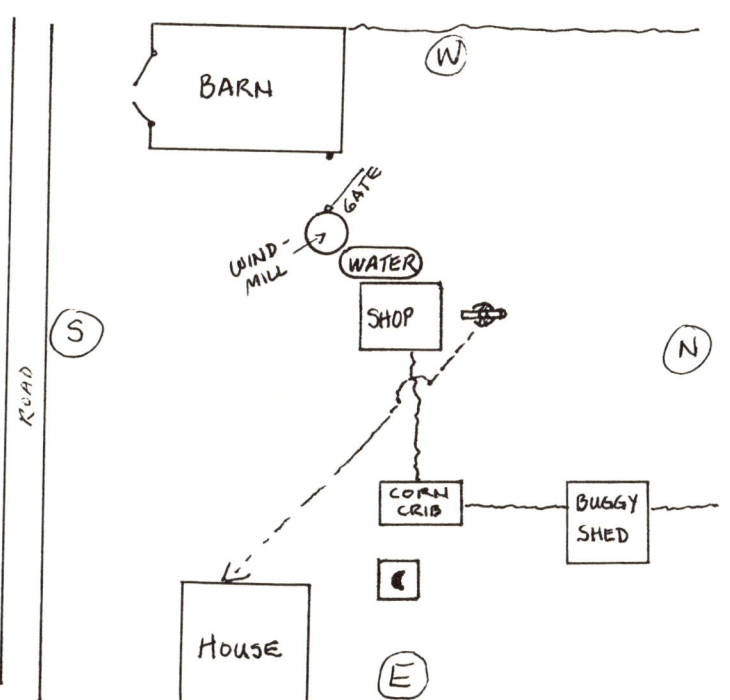

big boom. We waited about five minutes and nothing happened. We cautiously returned to the fence, looked through two knotholes and discovered the fuse had only burned to the first knot.

There was nothing to do but start over again. We got out the paper sack we used before, put in about six straws and each of us reached in and drew out one. I hoped I wouldn't get the short one this time, but I did. I had another concern this time, the fuse had burned to the knot and there was only a little of it left, real close to the cannon barrel which I knew would hurry me to get over the fence before it went off.

When Percy and I Built the Cannon

Percy used the same knothole as he used before as I took the match from my pocket, struck it with my shaking hand on a stone near the barrel and moved it cautiously toward the fuse. When it began to spit I high tailed it for the fence, put my hands over the top and at that moment the greatest explosion sounded that I have ever heard. It seemed like the whole earth shook and I never figured how I got over the fence. The explosion might have actually helped me over. After the big boom I realized I couldn't hear any sound.

I raced to the house where Percy stood like a petrified stone. On the way back I glanced over and saw cattle with tails straight up running in stampede fashion.

Mr. Doolittle came out of the barn in high gear making the first quick move in his life, with coat tails sticking straight out in back asking, "What happened!?" Percy replied in a nonchalant manner, "Oh, we just fired a cannon, that's all." Mr. Dolittle probably felt responsible for having two young whippersnappers shooting a cannon while their folks were away. After learning what took place he walked slowly and thoughtfully back in the barn to resume his chores.

Percy and I went back to the shop to see what had happened. We were amazed to find the back end of the shop blown out. We walked right through it. Dad's chopping block was split in many pieces and we never found any pieces of the cannon barrel, apparently it disintegrated into many pieces and blew away. Percy yelled loudly and finally got me to understand that we might have used too much powder. From the looks of the shop and the field piece we used I had to agree.

There was nothing we could do at the moment, so Percy went home and I went to the barn and found Mr. Dolittle feeding the cows. As I sat down on a milk stool to milk the cows I couldn't get my mind off my deafness. Before I finished milking, Dad came home from the fair. I told him about firing the cannon, the shop and my hearing loss. Dad said he would take me to see Dr. Haynes that night. The doctor examined me and thought I might get over it in a few days, and I did.

Dad thought Percy and I should fix the shop, which took us about a week after school. No mention was made of the chopping block and soon dad had a new apple wood block as good as the old one.

Mr. Dolittle was an old man then, but I believe firing the cannon speeded him up a bit.

I feel fortunate not to have been hit by a piece of steel from the explosion of the cannon barrel. The only scar that I will carry for life is a powder burn on the back of my right hand.

Chapter 20

WHEN EARL HAD THE MUMPS

Before the days of the corn binder, farmers planted corn in rows both ways. When it was ripe, it was cut by hand with a corn knife and stood on end in shocks to keep it dry. They would draw it into the barn or leave it in the field to husk the ears.

I wanted my little brother to do all the things I did, although he was six years younger. When he was ten years old, I was husking corn from the shocks in a field across the road from the house. I got him out there with me, but he fell asleep under a shock of corn and slept all afternoon. The next day he had a fever and mother called Dr. Haynes. The doctor didn't know what Earl had for a week and finally diagnosed it as mumps that had settled in his kidneys. He was put on a buttermilk diet for six weeks.

Mother was careful not to bake anything Earl could smell. But one day she decided to bake some cookies. He asked her to lay one next to his cot where he could see it. Later she came in his room. The cookie was gone and she said, "What happened to the cookie?" He said, "I ate it."

Chapter 21

THE RAILROAD TIES

Earl, Leonard and I went swimming by the high banks along the river one day late in August. While swimming, we noticed east of us and under the south bridge, some railroad ties stuck on a sandbar on the banks of the St. Joe River. We felt we had made a great find, for they could be made into anchor posts on the farm, especially when you wanted to put a gate between them.

A few days later a farmer stopped in front of the barn and said, "I have a claim on those railroad ties in the river." Later I talked to my father about the ties. He said, "I don't think he has a claim on the ties in the river. They must have belonged to the New York Central Railroad that crosses the St. Joe River. When the railroad company built the bridge they must have tossed the unwanted ones in the river below." So, Earl, Leonard and I floated them down the river about two miles, the way the river winds, to our section of the farm. There we hauled them up on the bank far enough so they would be secure.

We hooked Maud and Trilby on the stoneboat and hauled the ties to the house and laid them in a pile in our barnyard. We used them for anchor posts that lasted for many years.

Chapter 22

MY FATHER COULD DO ANYTHING WITH A HORSE

We had a horse by the name of Maud and she was about the orneriest critter that I ever met. Trilby, our other horse, was different. She was quiet and very nervous. If something would happen, she would start shaking all over.

One day my folks were gone and I expected to drill some oats. I harnessed Maud and Trilby to the drill. Things went along smoothly until Maud started acting up. She kicked over the drill tongue, kicked some more and broke loose from the harness, and went to the barn, leaving Trilby just standing there shivering. I drove Trilby to the barn and past Maud (watching out for the feet flying because she was still kicking).

We had a round oak stove being installed by the salesman, Herb Sinclair. He heard the rumpus in the barn and stopped to see what was going on. Mr. Sinclair was so angry with Maud kicking like she did that he stood and whipped her with the tugs on the harness until he was exhausted.

By that time dad came home. He went in beside Maud with no fear and brought his knee against her rib cage and she quieted down a bit.

There were horse traders going though the country at that time and there were as many as twenty or thirty horses tied together. I wanted to trade Maud off for another horse. I traded her for a little bronco. Dad shed a few tears and said she should be shot but never traded off. I had a buggy with a top on it that we kept in a shed at the end of the barn. I was anxious to hook the new horse up to see how she would act. Not thinking what would happen, I hooked her up and started to drive away. Instead of going forward as I planned, she backed right into the shed and broke the top right off! I finally got her to go ahead and eventually she made a good buggy horse.

Chapter 23

BUTCHERING THE PIG WITH BEN

Sometime around 1919 or 1920, my cousin Benjamin Wetherbee moved from Homer to the John Ballentine farm when Ben's father, Gibson, bought it. It was one half mile east of our farm. He was a town boy from the word go and hardly knew a pitchfork from a hoe. Within a few months he had a horse and saddle and rode everywhere he went. He raised pigs, drew manure, cultivated corn and all the things the average farm boy did. Ben's mother, Cary, was my cousin. Our mothers were sisters. Gibson, Ben's father, was a rural mail carrier, so most of the farm was worked on shares by surrounding farmers.

About a year after Wetherbees moved on the farm, Ben talked to me about a pig they had ready to butcher and asked me if I thought he could do it. He didn't have much equipment or experience, so I said, "I can help you next Saturday if you would like me to." So, we made a deal and set a date for the following Saturday.

I thought I should look at the hog and make a few plans, so we rode our horses down to see the hog. On arriving, we peered over the hogpen gate and Ben called the hog and she came stumbling out of the hog house. When I saw that big white sow, chills went down my spine. "That's a big pig," I called to Ben and added, "She'll weigh over two hundred." I began to have doubts about tackling the job, but I'd committed myself, so I didn't want to back out. I jumped on my horse and left with a parting reply, "See you Saturday!"

Butchering the Pig with Ben

Saturday was a cold, snowy, blustery day. I bundled up wearing my heavy mackinaw boots and wool stocking cap. I wrapped my butcher knives in part of an old cotton sheet, put my whetstone in my pocket and dragged the block and tackle behind me in the snow. On arriving, Ben had let the horses out in the barnyard and put the hog in the horse barn, which had four stalls. When I got in the barn and saw the space she had to run in, I was puzzled about how we could corral her, but we were too involved with other problems to dwell on it.

We decided to do our butchering in an old hen-house. We braved the blowing snow to carry water in pails from the well to a small iron kettle Ben had, and built a wood fire under it near the hen-house. The severe cold and blowing snow strengthened our decision to do our butchering in the hen-house where we would be more comfortable. We further decided to hang the hog up on the house joists using the block and tackle. The old joists had seen better days, but by putting a strong two-by-four across a number of joists, we agreed it should support the heavy hog.

These were the days before we skinned hogs, so we planned to scald and scrape it to remove all hair from the carcass. We resurrected an old wooden barrel that appeared to have been used for this purpose before, and placed sawhorses with planks on top near it so we would souse the hog in hot water by using the block and tackle.

Making all these preparations was taking a lot of time, so I said to Ben, "We're all set out here, so let's get that sow killed and strung up," whereby I grabbed my two razor sharp butcher knives and we headed for the horse barn where the pig was. When Ben opened the barn door we were surprised to find some of the harnesses knocked off the long wooden pegs back of the stalls. We could see without question that corralling that big hog was impossible in that large space. While contemplating what to do, the hog ran between Ben's legs and he went rolling onto the straw covered floor. As I looked about the barn I spied a piece of board fence large enough to cover the open end of a stall, and called to Ben, "How about using that short piece of fence to put against a stall to hold that rambunctious hog?" Ben thought it a good idea, but to get the animal in a stall was something else. Like a neighbor of ours said, "A hog has a head on both ends." We finally managed to get the board fence roped on one side of a stall, then swung it around against the wall of the barn. The pig, after a spell, ran into the stall and we slammed the fence shut and tied it securely.

Chapter 23

We stopped to get our breath and calculated our next move. Bleeding a hog is the part of butchering I didn't like, even though it is painless to the animal. But you don't hesitate on something that has to be done, so you do it. A hog has little to hang onto as they are so round and their nose and legs are tapered. It took all our strength to roll the hog over by grasping it legs. I straddled the front part of the hog where I could bleed it and Ben sat on the back with nothing to hang onto. The back legs of the hog were churning and the sharp hoofs went through Ben's overalls, underwear and some hide. As we dragged the killed hog over the snow to the henhouse, Ben complained about the circulating cold air in and around his rear end.

Filling the barrel with boiling water from the kettle was a hand-warming job. Hooking one end of the block and tackle to the joists and the other end to the hog didn't take long and we were ready to do the scalding. Lifting the hog over the barrel with the block and tackle made the hen-house building groan and creak. Ben guided the hog as I let the rope out to let it down, then we quickly grabbed the rope to raise the hog out of the hot water. We promptly lowered the hog, laid it on the planks and hooked the other end of the sow on the tackle and scalded the other end (as the barrel wasn't deep enough to scald the whole sow at one time). After scalding the other half, we raised the sow and let her down on the planks and both started scraping with the hog scrapers fast and furious. With a half hour of scraping, we had a nice clean hog. We hooked the block and tackle on the hog, raised it to a hanging position, removed the planks and sawhorses, and stood back to admire our work. The hot water on the frozen dirt floor had made about three inches of sloshy mud, but our boots took care of that and we knew it would freeze overnight.

We were getting ready to dress out the hog when we heard a splintering noise and looked up to see the joists give way one by one leaving the clean white hog laying in the mud. At that very moment Ben's grandma stuck her head in the door to see how we were getting along. She opened here mouth to speak, but never said a word. Ben did all the talking. He spoke with a firm conviction. "Grandma, we don't need your help. We don't need your advice.

Butchering the Pig with Ben

We can take care of everything. You can go right back in the house." Ben's grandma didn't say a word, which was unusual for her, then she closed the hen-house door and returned to the house.

Ben and I stood there disheartened as we looked at that fine hog laying in the mud. Soon we started looking the situation over and I said, "I think we could put some posts under those joists and again draw that hog up out of the mud using the block and tackle." In a short time we had some posts in place under the joists and the hog pulled up out of the mud. We scrubbed the hog down with warm water from the kettle until it looked white and clean. Things started looking better and again we felt on top of the situation.

While I dressed out the hog, Ben let the horses back in the barn, for it was a cold windy day. Later Ben brought me a dishpan to hold the heart, liver and tongue. I split the hog in half with my butcher knife and then finished splitting the carcass with a sharp axe.

We put out the fire under the kettle with snow. I put the whetstone in my pocket, wrapped my butcher knives in the old sheet I brought them in and started for home dragging my block and tackle behind me in the snow. I reflected on Ben's ventilated pants and was grateful it wasn't more serious. I took a more leisurely pace going home for we had had an exciting hard day.

School Days

Chapter 24

DARROW SCHOOL

My formal education started in a typical one room school in Clarendon Township, Calhoun County, Michigan. A number of generations of Clarendon children received their grade school education in this building. Its plain white rectangular shape, platform steps, with no shrubbery to subdue the harshness of the setting portrayed the character of the community that supported it: a hardworking, extremely practical agrarian society who saw no need for furnishing anything beyond the very basic needs. A wide strip around the school building devoid of grass where we played "Anti-I-Over" resembled a race track. A small baseball diamond, horse shoe court and the school pump occupied a sizeable part of the school grounds. Two pupil-made holes in the back board fence gave access to the farm fields and apple orchard where we played "Indian" with bows and arrows, roamed the hedgerows and enjoyed the abundant wild life. In the fall the tall corn and later the shocks furnished a hiding place for some of the big boys to get their homemade corn cob pipes and take a short smoke of corn silk.

The big trees that lined the road on both sides of the yard became part of us. It was in their shade we held our secret meetings away from the influence of the teacher. The big boys conducted the "affairs of state" under the guise of being democratic as every item taken up was voted on, but extreme pressures were put on the younger and less experienced on "how to vote." It was strictly understood that whatever went on at these gatherings was never to be revealed. The mores of the school preserved the success of the system: tattle-tale pupils quickly became unpopular and found it difficult to be accepted by their peers. These big trees challenged our climbing skills, tossed us in the wind at the further-most ends of their limbs, giving us a panoramic view of the surrounding farm land and buildings. It gave each one a few moments alone if he chose, to be with his own thoughts or time to spend with a small group where friendships often became close and lasting.

The front and only door to the school had a conspicuous solid brass handle and latch kept polished by constant use. The heft and extra width of the door made it slow to open. As you entered, the teacher's desk was near and at the left facing the room, and a recitation seat facing the desk held about twelve pupils. Individual pupil desks with varnished wood tops and ornamental cast iron frames were placed in rows and fastened to the floor facing the teacher ranging from small in front to large in back. Each had an inkwell, book storage and room for a slate and sponge.

A round oak wood burning stove, with a smoke pipe running up and to the back of the room to the chimney, with an ash scuttle and woodbox next to it was a prominent fixture in the center of the room. To the right of the door was a water pail and dipper on a bench with a wash basin, soap and linen towel. Individual drinking cups hung on the wall over the pail with the owners name by each hook. The built-in dinner pail cupboard with two screened doors for ventilation and protection from flies made adequate space on top for a globe, boxes of chalk and blackboard erasers.

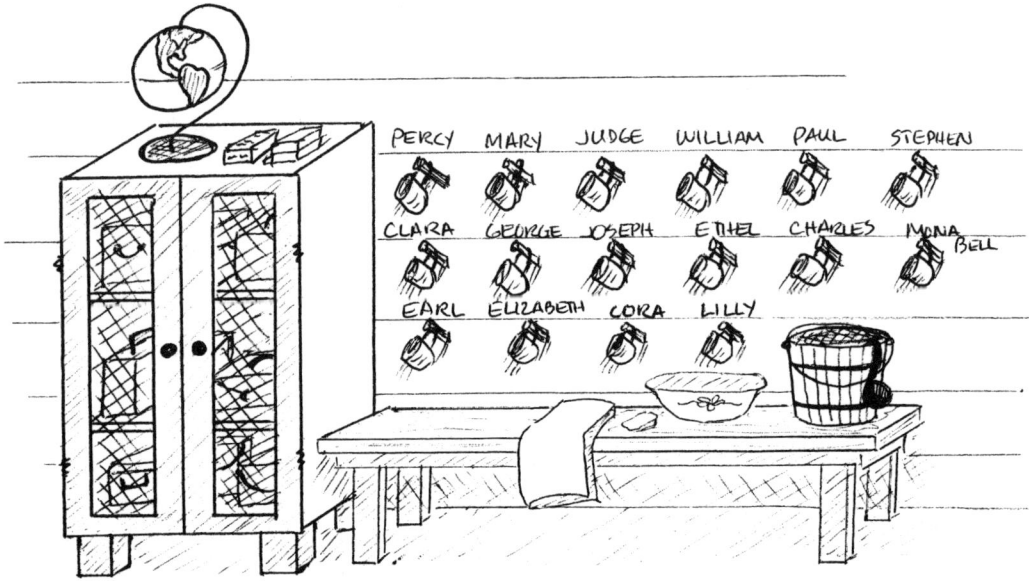

The library shelves in the corner beyond the water pail were filled with books from the revolving county library. A light gray paint covered the walls. The ceiling panels were solid white pine boards. Much of the light from the four big windows on both sides of the room was absorbed by the gray walls, but we seldom used the kerosene wall lamps.

Chapter 24

On dark, cloudy winter days we sometimes crowded two in a seat next to a window to see better. The windows had roller shades with strong springs that, when left down, would occasionally cut loose without warning, filling the room with a rushing sound, ending with a pistol-like report that brought some pupils standing with hands over their ears.

The back wall was lined with coat hooks kept filled with heavy wool clothes during the cold weather.

Miss Clark, our teacher, seemingly was at ease in any situation and had things under control. Her personal neatness, appropriate dress and positive bearing combined to make her a natural disciplinarian. He coal black hair, parted on the side, brushed and twisted into a bun on the back of her head, was held in place with a wide variety of decorative combs. This, combined with her dark brown eyes and olive complexion, enhanced her beauty. The simplicity of her dress, including her white blouse with narrow black tie, plain grey wool skirt, wool stockings and low heel shoes combined to give her particularly good looks.

Darrow School

Getting up and ready for school on cold winter mornings without running water and with wood burning stoves called for good organization. Mother and dad were up early buildings fires, doing chores and starting breakfast. The stairway door opened in our big farm house and my mother's voice penetrated the cold air in my bedroom announcing a new day. I lay there a minute tucked in between cotton sheets on a feather bed mattress with wool blankets over me, warm and cozy from my own body heat before I made the plunge into my cold bedroom where I slept with windows open. I grabbed my clothes, well organized the night before, and hurried down the stairs.

Dressing in front of the wood burning stove in the living room with the smell of brewed coffee, frying ham, cooked oatmeal and toast floating in from the kitchen range was a great way to start the day. Dad was soon in from doing chores and the four of us, Mother, Dad, my little brother Earl and I sat down together and waited for father to say grace before we ate. I had oatmeal, an egg and milk for my breakfast.

Breakfast over, my mother helped me get ready for the day in school. My dinner pail, originally an Ojibwa chewing tobacco box with a handle, was packed with a beef sandwich, two molasses cookies, a jar of milk and an apple. I chose to walk cross-lots rather than take the road to school, to check on rabbit runs in the snow in anticipation of some weekend hunting. As I approached the school I saw Percy climbing the fence. He waited for me to go with him behind the outhouse blind where we could talk in private. You see: I was in the seventh grade now and had six years of school experience behind me which gave me confidence and self assurance. Being thought of by our peers as belonging to the big boys we were expected to be leaders and left no doubt in their minds that we could handle any playground situation that might arise.

By nine o'clock everyone was present; some going into the school house on arrival to get out of the cold while others enjoyed the snow and cold and waited until the handbell was rung at 9:00 o'clock for school to start. I was one of the last ones to respond to the bell.

This school setting was to become a major part of my total environment for eight years. My teachers, associations with schoolmates, textbook studies and playground experiences had much to do with my beliefs, habits, attitudes and skills carried with me through life. Experiences with success and failure at all grade levels became part of the trials of growing up.

Darrow School

Homer High School

The "Meadola" I designed & built in Manual Training class

Class of '21

Bridge over St. Joe River

My first date with Dee

Chapter 25

THE CURRICULUM AT DARROW SCHOOL

Many early 20th century educators doubted that the one room rural school that bore such a prominent part in shaping our country ever had a counterpart. It had all the ingredients to give children a well-rounded experience for taking a place in the local community, but it took a good teacher to organize the whole school into a close-knit working unit to make it that way. Having children in all eight grades in one room under one teacher had some distinct advantages. It was a good learning situation for the bright, alert child in the lower grades who could profit by listening to and observing the upper grades recite and work at the blackboard. Children proficient in one or more subjects enjoyed exhibiting their knowledge by helping others -- with both those helping and those being helped benefitting. The quality of a school depended more on the innate ability of the instructor rather than her training, for only six weeks in a county normal school beyond high school was required by law for a license to teach and none of the teachers I had in rural school had more formal education than this.

As I look back at my early school experience I feel it had much to do with the kind of person I became. The examples set by my teachers, the close contacts with my peers, our games, textbooks and overall atmosphere set the stage for many of the attitudes, beliefs and aims in life that I hold today. Rural school children in our time lived close to nature and the soil, quite uncluttered by outside distracting influences and our limited resources, by necessity, made us practical and conservative. Working along side our parents on the farm, we knew where our food came from and appreciated the labor involved in producing it.

Our textbooks were geared to the social, economic, moral and political conditions of our generation. Arithmetic problems dealt with measurements of land areas, lumber, dry and liquid measurements frequently used by farmers and merchants. Our history books pictured our national life in a way that justified every action ever taken by our country. I grew up with a feeling of absolute security under the American flag and felt proud to be a citizen of the United States believing my country would be honorable in dealing with other countries and protect its people under all circumstances. Current events were included in our Social Studies once a week for seventh and eighth graders. They appeared to have little meaning for those whose families took no newspapers and had no contacts with the world outside their immediate community. I well remember one current event I gave telling about an invention by a man named Marconi that made it possible to send messages without wires. I got some good laughs from those who thought I was trying to be funny and the teacher didn't seem to comprehend its possibilities and said it wasn't a very good current event.

The map and descriptions of the countries found in our geography books seemed more fictitious than real to us. Our conception of long distances and the world were made shallow by our confinement to our community . . . some never having ventured beyond their county line. When I was in the sixth grade, I took a trip with my mother to visit my aunt. We went by train to Detroit, then took a paddle wheel steamer named "City of Cleveland" across Lake Erie to Buffalo and Niagara Falls. Returning to school I was hailed as a traveler of note and besieged with requests to tell them the story of my trip.

Language Arts was divided into reading, orthography, spelling, grammar and literature, with a text for each of these subjects. All stories in our readers had a moral theme encouraging such ideals as honesty, thrift, loyalty, patriotism and consideration of others. I well remember the stories about George Washington who never told a lie and honest Abe Lincoln. The story "The Ball of String" depicted an

Chapter 25

exciting bow and arrow shooting match where both contestants broke their bow strings. One contestant had thoughtfully saved pieces of string and came to the match with them in his pocket enabling him to restring his bow and win the match. Then there was that well-known story of Midas and his gold who selfishly hoarded it, never using it to help others. Finally, everything he touched turned to gold, even the food he picked up to eat, and it destroyed him.

Considerable emphasis was put on the proper spelling and pronouncing of words. A separate test book on orthography was used to teach us the rules of spelling, which we were required to memorize. A companion spelling book containing the most commonly used words, with definitions and examples of their use in sentences, was included with many exercises and problems for us to work. One method used for memorizing these words was to write them fifty or a hundred times. This exercise didn't seem to work too well for me as I had my mind on more interesting things during my writing and ended up still unable to spell the word. Each Friday we had spelling bees and most of the kids worked to prepare for it. On parents' night we sometimes competed with a team of adults. These spelling bees were great fun, stimulating and productive.

It took considerable discipline on the part of the kids from Darrow School to master the grammar we were required to study. Language usage in a community like ours with its colloquial terms and expressions and the influences of the ethnic groups made Standard English difficult to master. The proper sequence of words, made into sentences in a way to give them meaning, was the basic aim of the author of our textbook. We memorized the parts of speech and learned how to construct simple and compound sentences by diagramming them, which was a graphic method of analyzing a sentence used by schools at that time. This method seemed to work well for the serious student and was a fine preparation for High School English. It appeared to be of little help to the slow or disinterested pupil where eighth grade terminated their education.

Literature wasn't given a prominent place in our curriculum. Our county traveling library was inadequate; besides, there were few books written for school-age children in the early part of the twentieth century.

The Curriculum at Darrow School

So, much of our school day was taken up with drill work and memorization and it left little time for free reading and literary study. Each year the State Superintendent of Public Instruction selected one poem that all eighth grade pupils were required to study and be tested on in May.

Our education wasn't considered complete unless we could write legibly. Hours were spent practicing penmanship -- care being taken to see that the school desk was adjusted for height, body erect, feet flat on the floor and the pen held properly. Much of our writing in school was done on our slates, but paper was felt necessary for penmanship as we had to master the steel pen, which required a very special skill. We were taught to use our arms and not our fingers for better control to form letters, and regulate the pressure of the sharp pointed pen on the paper so it wouldn't cut through it. We used the Spencer Method of Writing, not only to encourage legibility, but for the beautiful formation of letters as well. There was lively competition between pupils, and admiration of those who acquired proficiency in penmanship. Most of the teachers I had were good penmans and put exercises for us to copy on the big slate boards that extended across the front of the school room. Writing well on the blackboard required a skill quite different than with pen and paper. Kids grouped around the board at recess and noon time on bad weather days to improve their slate board writing.

Aa Bb Cc Dd Ee Ff Gg

Agriculture could have been considered as a vocational subject, for nearly all of the pupils in our school came from farm families. I remember learning little from it, probably because I saw it practiced at home and felt I knew all about it. It was not a challenging subject for me.

The subject of Physiology and Health was popular with most of the pupils in our school. Our association with heavy farm work instilled in us the importance of strong bodies capable of rigorous and long exposure to hard physical labor. We prided ourselves on having good muscle tone, endurance and skill and were willing to do whatever necessary to give us all of these. Our interest in healthful foods, exercise and rest, as we understood it at that time, came as a natural desire to be healthy. The time spent on Physiology and Health depended largely on the importance that the teacher we had at the time gave it. The teachers I had

Chapter 25

emphasized health. The result was that I followed the rules to the letter, and often to the extreme. For example, I slept all winter with one window of my bedroom removed for fear I might contract tuberculosis. I must have been super sensitive to be so concerned about the diseases we studied. I never discussed it with anyone, but worried about it unduly. However, the benefits I received from the study of Physiology and Health greatly outweighed the worries it caused me.

Music was taught from *Pat's Pick*, a book written by a Mr. Pattengill, a former County Commissioner of Schools. It had just the words of the songs without music. We opened school in the morning by repeating the "Pledge of Allegiance" to the flag followed by singing. Some of my teachers could play the reed pump organ, but if there was no one to play it, we sang acappella. Many pupils had favorite songs and made requests to be sung. I remember my favorite was "Yield Not to Temptation." I don't recall anyone who played an instrument in school. There were a few who were fairly good on the mouth organ, and sometimes they played while we sang from the *Knapsack Songbook*. People in our community had to be proficient in figures to succeed. Most families were in business for themselves, like farmers and merchants who had to know how to figure to survive. It is understandable that arithmetic had a high priority in our school as it did throughout the nation.

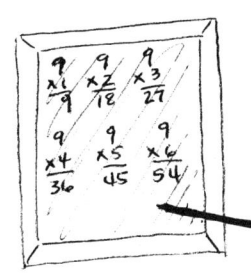

We were required to memorize the multiplication tables through the nines, know how to subtract numbers, learn combinations of numbers for adding columns and be proficient in short and long division by the time we finished the eighth grade. Our thick arithmetic book was full of practical story problems that dealt with linear, volume and distance measurements. Our textbooks were bought at Woodbury's Drug Store in Homer. Some were handed down from older brothers or sisters in the family or bought from older students who were through with it. Woodbury's also sold used books that students had traded in on new books.

A few students took excellent care of their books, but many were in poor shape. Pencil marks were found underlining paragraphs or words the particular boy or girl thought important to remember. Youngsters in our school also had the habit of writing in the inside covers of the books and drawing grotesque pictures, then putting a friend's name under it. If you had a text filled with names and drawn pictures, you had occasion to be proud.

Chapter 26

HIDE THE WHIP

    Play and activities outside our formal school day was an important part of our over-all education. Periods before school, fifteen minutes recess forenoon and afternoon, and the noon hour gave us ample time for recreation. Some of the games we played were handed down by our forefathers, others we invented and were peculiar to our school. Children naturally separated themselves into age groups for some games, but all were included in most of them. We took pleasure devising games that required courage, skill, strength, and agility. This separated the weak and meek from the courageous and strong. Peer pressure was ever present and many a kid entered into the rough games with great fear, but proud of his bravery.

    Hide-the-Whip was played in the spring when the thick grass next to the fences and in the fields made good places to hide the horse whip. Some kid on the playground, or just when school was out for recess or noon, would holler, "first one to put his hand in the hole is 'it'." This would start a stampede to put your hand in the hole in the siding on the back of the school house. (I never knew how the hole got there or how it got broken out each time it was fixed.) The first one to get his hand in the hole ran to get the horse whip from the school house while everyone else gathered on the front stoop out of sight of the whip hiding places. When the whip was hid, the leader would yell, "Come and get it!" triggering a scrambling mass of kids, full speed ahead, each bent on finding the whip. The finder could whip as many as he could catch before they got off limits on the front stoop. Some kids went helter skelter over a large area where we often hid the whip, while the more experienced watched the others, then methodically covered the most likely spots, all the time keeping in position to get back without getting hit with the whip.

    When the whip was located outside the playground, the high board fence with one small hole in it gave the finder a tremendous advantage. Small kids couldn't scale the fence and the hole in the fence admitted only one at a time, giving the whipper time to lick a lot of kids before they could get away. We used high quality whips capable of inflicting painful punishment in the hands of an aggressive pupil.

Hide the Whip

Discarded buggy whips were easily obtained from our homes as many of our fathers bought new style ones before the old ones wore out.

(A rig with a trotting horse, silver decorated leather harness and hand-striped buggy wasn't complete without a flashy whip.) Cutting them down from six to four feet and preserving the lashes on the business end made them easy to hide and a formidable flogging machine. Many a blistered leg came from being struck with a whipcord.

I remember asking my mother for my winter underwear in October. She said, "What on earth do you want long underwear this early for? You will roast wearing it in this weather." "I know," I said, "but they are playing Hide-the-Whip at school and I've got to wear it." Mother got it out reluctantly and it proved to be hot and uncomfortable, but great for softening those whip lashes.

Painful punishment could be inflicted with those whips by a big kid, but restraint was most always used. However, occasional grudges were resentfully taken out on someone they didn't like. Harold, three years my senior, seemed to take delight beating the daylights out of me whenever he got me off by myself in the field or in the boys' outhouse. Whenever he was around me he was like a

Chapter 26

throbbing toothache to me. During one of our games, many of us had crawled through the hole in the back fence in search of the hidden whip. I soon spied it, walked over to it with a poker face, waiting for more to get near it, bettering my chance to whip more kids before they could get away. My pulse quickened as I got closer to it. The minute I slid the whip from under the long lopped grass, everyone made a mad rush for the hole in the fence, but Harold was there first, so others started over the top. Harold caught his suspenders in a split board and in his haste, got hopelessly hung up. I had a perfect target with his pants tightly stretched over his buttocks sticking through my side of the fence. As I lashed away with the whip all the kids Harold had harassed in the past started yelling, "Let him have it!" After a minute of this, something told me, "this is enough." Harold soon got loose and started for me fired with rage, his face flushed and his red hair blown down over his eyes. I was ready to run when Judge Burns hopped over the fence, grabbed Harold by the shirt collar and said, "No you don't." Harold knew all about Judge's powerful body, his ability to fight and the respect his peers had for him, so he walked back into the field away from the rest of us as we resumed our game.

FOOTNOTE:

Harold, an adopted boy, accidentally set fire to his parent's barn when he was six years old. From then on he wasn't accepted by his family and became a poorly adjusted youth, misunderstood by his schoolmates and some people of the community. He enlisted in the army in WWI. I got his address and corresponded with him and through our exchange of letters, I got to feel a closeness to him and I believe he felt the same toward me. He was mortally wounded in Germany and died six weeks later in an Army hospital.

Chapter 27

PLAYING INDIAN

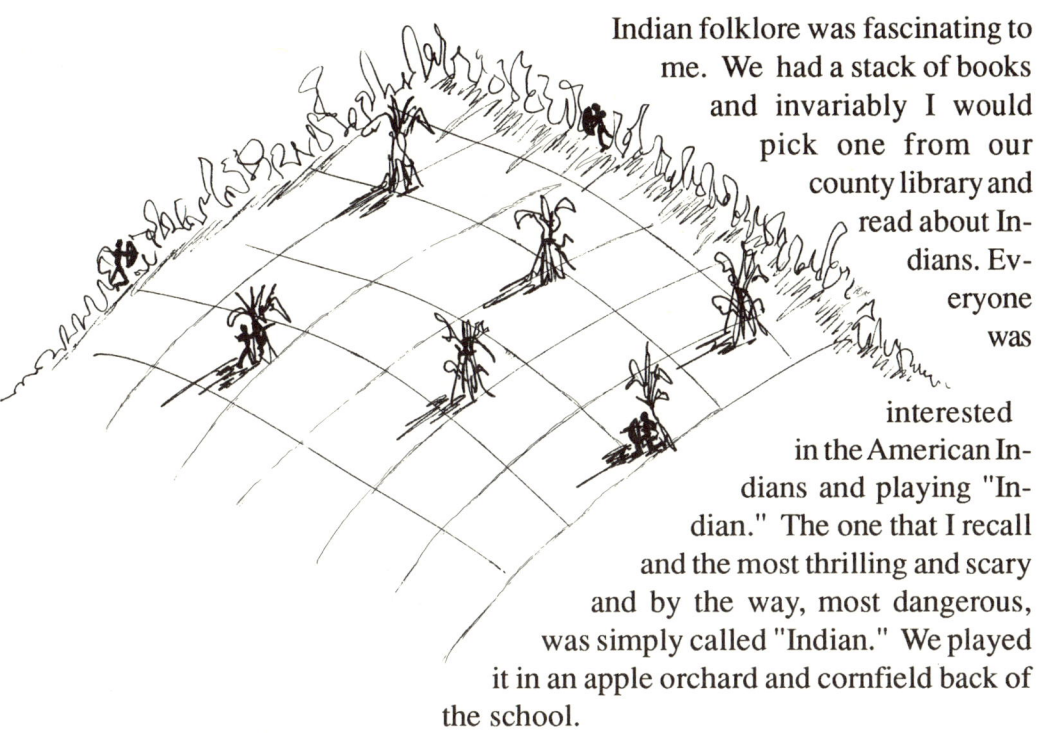

Indian folklore was fascinating to me. We had a stack of books and invariably I would pick one from our county library and read about Indians. Everyone was interested in the American Indians and playing "Indian." The one that I recall and the most thrilling and scary and by the way, most dangerous, was simply called "Indian." We played it in an apple orchard and cornfield back of the school.

When a field was planted to corn in rows 30 inches apart both ways, it served as a grid for designating a spot to meet a friend who, for example, might give his position as 28 rows south and 10 rows east from the Big Oak Tree.

At harvest time the farmer would cut the corn 20 hills square and stand it on end and bind it into a shock with binder twine. These shocks made a great buffer to hide behind. Both orchard and field were surrounded by hedges made up of small trees and brush perfect for ambush.

We played the game with bows and arrows. The bows could be made of seasoned hickory or sassafras and the arrows from cattail stalks. My father would form our bows from seasoned hickory that he split from small logs clamped in a vice and formed them into shape with a spoke shave. The cattails for our arrows were allowed to dry in the house.

Playing Indian

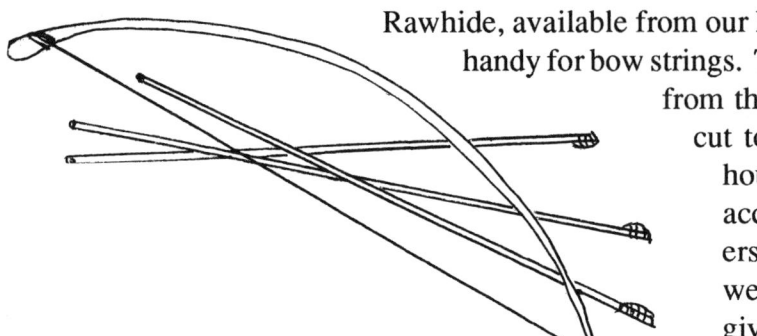

My father patiently taught me to make my own bows and his tools were always available to me without asking. The seasoned wood bows were as stiff as steel and drove the arrow with lightning speed. Rawhide, available from our harness shop, was always handy for bow strings. The cattails were gathered from the marshes in the fall and cut to length and dried in the house. They were not as accurate, for we hadn't feathers for them. But we put a weight in the leading edge to give them stability in flight.

I played my first game of Indian when I was in the fifth grade. John Matson and Judge Burns were eighth graders, self-appointed leaders, who announced we would play the next day at noon. I had lived for the day when I would be big enough to play Indian. Now that the time had come, I experienced moments of great anxiety knowing I would be battling some experienced Warriors. On my way to school with my bow and crude quiver filled with arrows over my back and dinner pail in hand, I tried to envision the tough situation I might encounter and how I might handle it when the time came. I had the practical experience of shooting arrows into the straw stack, hitting the mark reasonably well, but I realized it would be more difficult to shoot accurately when I had to be on the look-out right and left to avoid getting hit by an arrow in the back.

As the clock hour hand neared twelve, pupils at their seats started to put their desk in order in preparation for the noon hour. The instant the teacher hit the desk bell, everyone was under motion grabbing their dinner pails and heading for the sunny side of the school house out of the wind. The grass was dry next to the building so that's where we ate our lunch. It only took a few minutes to eat for we practically swallowed our lunches without chewing in order to get started with our games.

John and Judge took turns selecting players until all were chosen into two tribes. I, being inexperienced, was one of the last chosen. To designate which tribe each of us was in, Judge had brought bright red feathers from Rhode Island Red rooster tails for the "Reds" to wear in their caps and white feathers from Plymouth

Chapter 27

Rock roosters for the "Whites." We drew cuts for position and the Red Tribe got south hedge row and the White got the north. Our Reds had the poorest hedge row with the least trees and brush, but we were nearest to the cornfield filled with rows of corn shocks.

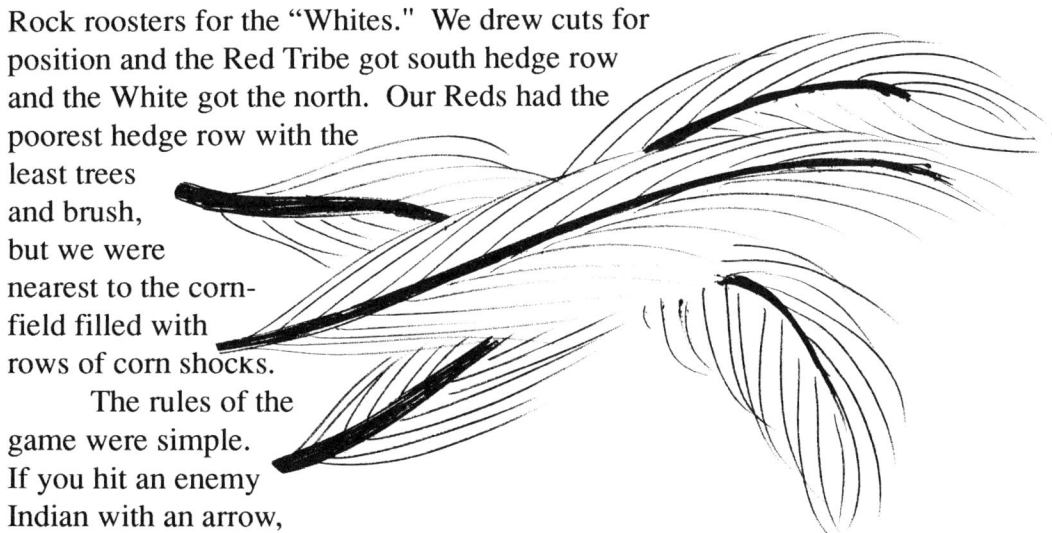

The rules of the game were simple. If you hit an enemy Indian with an arrow, he was considered dead and out of the game. If you could sneak up and touch him he was considered scalped and out of the game. We played until all of one tribe were killed or scalped. If the bell rang before one side won we started the next day where we left off.

The game was well under way. I quickly pulled my bow string taught and aimed it toward a noise I heard. As the sound came nearer, my heart went THUMP, THUMP, THUMP! Just as I was about to shoot, our tribe leader, Judge, came into view. He was working his way among our Red Tribe members to circle behind the Whites and get them to surrender.

The Reds took cover in the south hedge squatting behind small trees out of sight. I was amazed at the quietness there, having expected immediate and intensive activity. There was a small breeze and the sounds of small children playing on the school grounds came drifting to us with the wind.

I spied Paul about two rows away, biting his lip and spitting every few seconds as he examined his bow and I wondered what he might be thinking. As I watched him I was startled to hear small twigs crashing underfoot. I turned and waited with bow in position. The brush parted and it was Judge giving Reds instructions to circle in behind the Whites and launch a surprise attack from the rear. I decided to crawl to the first apple tree where I could get a better view in the open. I made it to the tree, a big one with a large trunk giving me good protection. I got myself organized with arrow notched in bow string and decided to peer out to see if it looked clear enough to try for the next tree. I stuck my face about a head's width

Playing Indian

beyond the tree trunk and WHOOSH! I felt the whiff of an arrow coming inches from my nose as it sped by. I decided my position was dangerous and the corn shocks might give me more protection if I could maneuver around to them. Going back by the way of the hedge seemed the best route. The grass was deep for ten feet from the trees so I planned to crawl through it in a bent-over position, then run the rest of the way, about fifty feet to the hedge. I tied my bow under the quiver strap on my back and started crawling quietly at a turtle's pace to avoid being spied. I made it through the grass unnoticed, then broke into a run. I realized my mistake as the arrows whizzed by me. I decided to keep on until I reached the hedge. I saw the Whites coming from all angles. The thought came to me, "Maybe we're being ambushed!!"

I reasoned the Whites were closing in on us and I could improve my position by moving to the other end of the cornfield. The close calls with arrows made me wiser and more cautious as I worked my way back to the other end of the cornfield. Again, I faced wide open spaces. To reach the first shock I would have to travel about fifteen feet. The experiences in the last few minutes and the thought of crossing that open area readied my body for it. As I got in position at the edge of the opening I could hear my heart beat like horses' feet on hard ground.

I dug a depression with my heel in the hard clay, got in position, looked right and left and dove ahead. Instantly I was in bad trouble. A dead limb hooked the strap on my back, threw me to the ground, and spilled my arrows over a broad area. Before I could think what to do, Percy emerged from the hedge, surveyed the field deliberately, and like a brave story-book character, picked up my arrows. He returned them to me so I would have some arrows in case I needed them. Now he shoved me toward the center of the field. I made it to one of the center shocks and crawled underneath it so I wouldn't be out in the open. By using some force, I could pry the stalks apart and see in all directions.

While I was getting situated I could hear footsteps. I dared not open the stalks for fear I would be heard. So I waited. Then a foot appeared by the opening I had made crawling into the shock. I didn't recognize the foot so I didn't know whether it belonged to a "Red" or "White." If I grabbed it and it was a White, it would be considered as an enemy scalped. If it was a Red I might upset his plans so I remained silent and he moved on.

I felt secure in the corn shock, hidden and insulated from the enemy's arrows but I had a feeling of being alone and without direction. I was getting in the mood to leave the shock and roust some White feathered Indians when I heard some loud yelling. I jumped out in the open in time to see all the Whites charging across the

Chapter 27

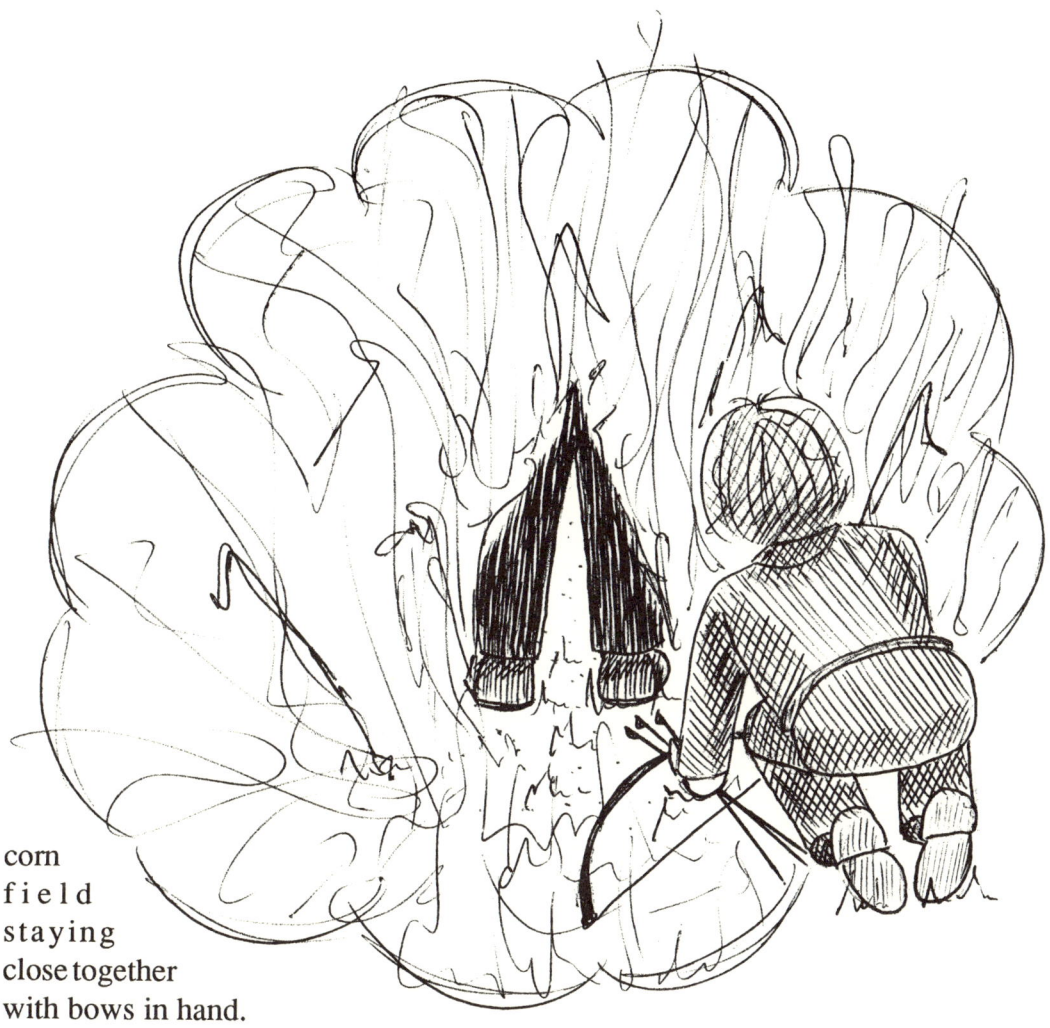

corn
field
staying
close together
with bows in hand.

The Reds started popping up here and there, both sides yelling and the arrows started flying. They were getting close. I drew my bow and aimed it hurriedly and let the bow string slip from my fingers. It missed a White by inches. I raised my right arm and moved sideways like lightning to let an arrow miss me. I ducked behind a shock for protection when an arrow just missed my shoulder and stuck in the shock. I turned to find its source and a White was almost on me. I didn't have a chance. He put his hand on me and I was "scalped" and out of the game. I ran back and sat on the fence to see our Reds shot or scalped one by one. We had just time enough to hang our bows on hooks over our name inside the 'backhouse stockade' when the school bell called us back to the books.

Chapter 28

TRADING THE WATCH

The day started with noisy enthusiasm and intense activity. There were dinner pails to be put away, coats and boots to take off and hang on hooks in the back of the room and much to talk about. There were always helping hands and a spirit of cooperation without which a rural school couldn't be run. (Lord, have mercy on the one room rural school teacher that wasn't well organized.) Teaching all eight grades, eleven subjects -- reading, writing, arithmetic, history, geography, agriculture, health and music -- and doing the janitorial work on less than $50 a month called for dedication and careful planning. A sense of pride, accomplishment and skill motivated pupils to take responsibility for doing useful jobs around the school.

Paul was in demand as a pencil sharpener because he was considered the best in school. He had a Keen Kutter jackknife honed to a razor's edge on an Arkansas stone and finished off on his father's razor strop. He would often test its edge by shaving hair off the back of his hand. Pupils stood in line by his desk in the morning for a pencil sharpening; the prudent ones specifying blunt leads to lessen the chance of breakage; the less conservative calling for long sharp pointed leads for finer writing. Paul liked the five cent Velvet pencils over the penny ones as their fine grained white pine hexagon shaped varnished wood lent itself to a masterful job.

Judge Burns, an eighth grader, was as accurate as a modern thermostat. He could sense the slightest change in room temperature from his seat in the back of the room and would immediately walk quietly to the stove to adjust the damper or draft, shake the grate or add wood. Even with all of Judge's skill in operating the stove it was humanly impossible to keep those next to the stove from becoming too warm and those on the room perimeter from being cold. We learned to add and take off clothes to compensate for the differences.

All our activities outside the formal school program were made up of games handed down from generations before us or of our own invention. We had few ways to make money and there wasn't much of it floating around anyway so one of the activities that took much of our time was trading things of small value. If you could start out with an old "toad-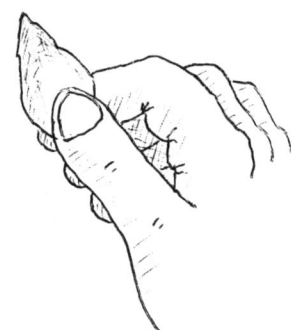stab" of a jackknife and, through lively trading for a year, end up with an old Clipper bicycle with solid rubber tires you were recognized as a good "horse-trader."

I had access to a relatively unusual commodity given to me by my older brother, Lynn, who worked for a jeweler. He brought me old discarded watches, mostly what we referred to as "dollar watches" and showed me some of the rudimentary steps for dismantling them and putting them back together. I was able to get many of them running and put the movements under a clear glass tumbler on my desk at school. I realized my objective when groups of kids gathered around my desk in the morning before school and during the noon hour fascinated by the running watch works and making attractive propositions for trading.

School was well under way on a fall morning in late November. The first grade occupied the recitation seat reading from their *Baldwin Readers*. Other pupils were working at their desks, using the library or helping others with their lessons. A low din from those reciting, student helpers and the crackling of the wood fire filled the room. The mingling of smells from the heavy clothes and boots in the back that had hung in ham smoked kitchens and worn around the animal barns gave off an aroma found nowhere else except in a rural schoolhouse.

George Ballentine, a year behind me in school, looked the teacher's way, raised four fingers (a request to speak to another pupil). The teacher nodded affirmatively and George came to my desk announcing his interest in my watch works. I was quick to get out my big geography book, stand it on edge on my desk opened, to give us some privacy. George lost no time in revealing the purpose of his mission as he reached in his pocket and took out a new Keen Kutter jackknife and whispered, "I'll trade this even for the watch works." My answer was a slow but sure "No," a rule I learned early about barter -- you never accept the first offer. George's father and uncle ran a general store and grain elevator in Clarendon, a town of ten houses on the New York Central Railroad, one half mile from the school. I suspected George had taken the jackknife from the store but knowing he waited on customers and had free access to the unlocked cases gave it little thought. Miss Clark, our teacher, apparently thinking I had helped George (with his geography) long enough motioned him back to his seat.

    George was at my desk again at noon and I could tell the more he saw the watch the greater his desire to have it. I sensed I was in a seller's market and should hold out for a big deal. Finishing our lunch George said, "Let's go outdoors where we can talk." We donned our heavy coats, wool stocking caps and went down under the big oak tree where there was a crude shelter, big rocks to sit on and, above all, privacy. It was then that George surprised me by producing the second Keen Kutter jackknife from his pants pocket and saying, "I'll trade you both knives for the watch works." I hesitated for a moment with the thought that this is a good deal and I had never had a knife of this quality before, but George was still hot and I ended up saying, "No." As we walked back to the school George gave me some good sales talks, then the bell rang and we went inside, hung up our coats and returned to our seats. George had to stay after school to make up some work, so I saw no more of him that day. I put the watch works in the small box in my dinner pail for protection, my arithmetic book in my knapsack for my homework and headed cross lots for home.

    Preoccupation with the watch/knife deal interfered with my homework. I was constantly alternating between taking or not taking George's offer. I had other watch works I was sure I could get running so I wouldn't be left without more trading stock, but the possibilities of a better proposition by George intrigued me. I went to bed that night with it on my mind. On waking the next morning, it was still there asking for a final decision.

    The next morning I walked to school with Ethel, a neighbor girl in my grade and one of my best friends. We didn't hurry and talked about the possibility of

Trading the Watch

playing "Fox and Geese" and other games using tracks in the snow but decided it wasn't deep enough, yet. As bad as I wanted to talk to Ethel about the trading business with George I decided against it. I considered it a private matter and good business to keep it between us two . . . besides, who knows, I might be offered a better proposition by someone else any time now. Ethel was a "slow poke" and we were almost late for school. The bell was ringing as we entered the yard giving us just time enough to put our dinner pails, coats and boots away. Even with the rush to get my things put away and get to my seat I did take time to get the box holding the watch works from my dinner pail and place it on my desk under the glass tumbler. The school day was soon under way in earnest and I found myself with our seventh grade class up front reciting for the teacher.

During time between recitation classes, hands showing one finger for permission to go to the backhouse, two to get a drink, three to see the teacher and four to see another pupil were in the air. Miss Clark made quick decisions on each and was back at her desk in minutes. I was surprised she gave George permission to see me. I knew it was about the big deal and I sensed the time had come for positive action. My pulse was fast. I had little idea what George was thinking. As I was taxing my decision-making faculties to the limit I proceeded to get out my big geography book and get it in place. I had an ideal location in the room, screened in front by the big book and a back seat with no one behind me.

I fully expected George to come forth with the two new Keen Kutter knives and review his previous offer which I had decided to accept, but again, he took me completely by surprise. He reached in his pocket and produced three new knives and said, "I'll give you three knives for the watch works." I stared out the window for a moment, fiddled with my inkwell cover, handled the three knives and then deliberately said, "Well, O.K., I'll trade."

Chapter 28

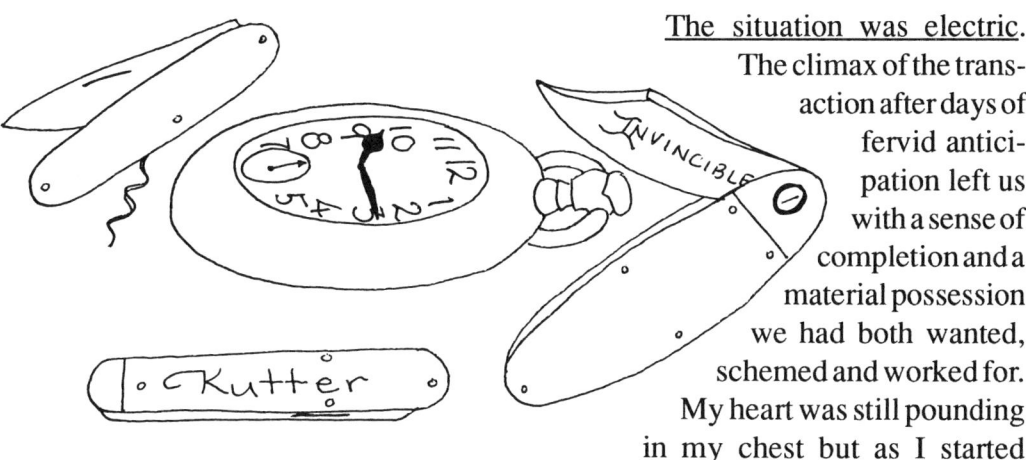

The situation was electric. The climax of the transaction after days of fervid anticipation left us with a sense of completion and a material possession we had both wanted, schemed and worked for. My heart was still pounding in my chest but as I started whispering to George I quieted down. I had heard from some of the other boys that George wanted to take watches apart and put them back together like I did. He was impulsive, undisciplined, with no knowledge about mechanical things. I knew I must show him how to care for his newly acquired works and keep him from spoiling it. I whispered to him, "If you ever decide to take the watch apart, let me show you how first. Don't ever loosen the screws on the plates before you unwind the main spring." I took my sharp pencil and pointed to the rachet and click that held it in a wound position. I showed him how to hold the watch movement firmly in the left hand with thumb and index finger gripping the stem before releasing the main spring click. "It's a tricky thing to do, George, I'll see you at noon then you can come to my house tonight so I can show you more." I was relieved when he showed interest in getting my help before experimenting. As he moved quietly unnoticed back to his seat I fondled the three shiny new jack knives, admiring the bone handles, brass linings, Keen Kutter trademark set in flush with the handles and the superb workmanship as I slipped them into my pocket before removing my geography book and placing it in my desk. The old oak wall clock read 9:30 -- one hour before morning recess. Switching from trading to school work came with considerable effort but the hour's work before dismissal seemed short.

    As I joined the ones who chose to go outside I noticed a group huddled around George to look at the watch and get the end results of the trade. Charles Matson, on seeing my three jackknives said, "Gee whiz, man, you struck it rich!" He was already pressing me for a trade for one of the knives but I needed time to think about it. It went through my mind that I should keep Charlie on my list as a trader, he being the son of the Clarendon blacksmith would have access to some good trading stock.

Trading the Watch

The school bell brought kids from all directions up on the open porch to remove boots and go inside as Miss Clark checked to see that no one tracked in dirt. I helped Mona Bell, a fourth grader, with her arithmetic then settled down at my desk to do my own studying. It was a quiet time after recess, the children having spent some of their physical energy at play and now were in the mood to do their schoolwork. A small class was reciting for the teacher and the others were working at their seats. The steady strong tick of the clock could be heard above the children reciting, the shuffle of heavy leather shoes on the wood floor and the soft low pitch sounds of the wind around the windows. There seemed to be no explanation why everyone would be quiet on some days and restless on others. This seemed to be one of those quiet days. Then in an instant **all heck broke loose**. We were startled by a high pitched whirring sound that broke into the still atmosphere. A girl screamed as a flying object hit her face. The room seemed filled with spinning, buzzing things. Some covered their faces. What I thought might happen, and hoped wouldn't happen, had happened. George had removed the screws from the watch plates without first unwinding the main spring.

A well organized day had turned into one of confusion and excitement. We weren't put back to work, instead, Miss Clark perched herself on the edge of a student desk next to the center of the room and used the situation to teach us some things about everyday living. We talked about things that made us happy and the importance of good judgement in different situations. We were soon relaxed and returned to our morning schedule.

George never found all the parts and some were broken beyond repair. I looked George's way -- he had his head cradled in his arms on his desk with a box full of motionless watch parts beside him.

Chapter 29

SMOKING

I can't remember the first conrcob pipe I ever saw. I grew up with them all around me as quite a few farmers used them.

Any kid interested in smoking could find all the needed materials in a cornfield; the cobs for the pipe bowl, dried silk for burning and the shocks to hide behind. I was introduced to smoking by my neighbor, Percy, as we walked to school together. We went crosslots as usual. As we sauntered between rows of tall corn, Percy whipped out a corn cob pipe he had made and explained, "It won't take you long to make one. Knock off a length of cob an inch and a half long and cut the fine chaff off the outside with your jackknife and finish it smoothly. Cut a basswood twig about

five inches long and pick the pith out of the center with a piece of fence wire, peel off the bark and you have a stem. Then whittle the stem to fit. You must clean out the soft pithy core of the cob, but be sure to leave the bottom closed." Instructions complete, Percy started looking at the thick silk at the top of the ears to find one that was sufficiently dry to burn properly. He found one and proceeded to load his pipe. He had trouble with his wooden matches (safety matches hadn't been invented yet). Most of the matches had gathered moisture and wouldn't light, but he finally got one to light by scratching the match on a dry stone. I watched with fascination but with a sense of fear at this new experience. Percy held the lighted match over the pipe bowl and took a drag and puffed. The air around us was filled with deep heavy smoke. Finishing, he rapped the ashes of his pipe against a stone and put the pipe in a paper sack (to seal the pungent odor) before

Smoking

placing it in his pocket. A pipe charred with burnt corn silk has a penetrating odor second only to skunk's oil and almost impossible to hide. When I got inside the school that morning I smelled like a bunch of burned leaves and wondered if anyone would notice it. I was ready with an explanation, but didn't have to use it.

I never scrutinized them until I started searching for one to use for a pipe. As I moved about the barn doing my daily chores, I went to the place where I could find cobs that had all the corn removed from them. We fed our horses and pigs corn on the cob, so I examined the cobs in the horses feed boxes. I ended up finding the best cob under our hand-cranked corn sheller with the big flywheel where we shelled corn on rainy or snowy days.

Both my father and mother had talked to me about their hope that I wouldn't acquire the tobacco habit. I rationalized that smoking corn silk was different than tobacco, but I still had a guilty feeling as I went about working secretly making my pipe. The cob I selected was of good quality from a fully matured ear, well dried, and it finished up nicely. I had it completed in a few days -- ready to take to school the next day.

A ray of sunlight entered my bedroom window the next morning announcing a new day, late in October. It didn't take long to dress, do chores, and eat breakfast with my mother, dad and little brother, Earl. I left for school early, anxious to show my pipe. It was a beautiful morning with air so clean and crisp you wanted to breathe it all in. Heavy frost had turned the ripe corn brown and some of the farmers had started cutting it.

Climbing the rail fence, entering our lane, I got a glimpse of a cotton tail who had been out all night and hadn't settled down for his day's sleep. Nearing the end of the lane, I heard a familiar honking noise from up above and watched a flock of Canada Geese fly overhead. I laid flat on my back on a patch of dry grass to get a better view of the gander leading his flock in a 'V' formation. I never watched big birds fly without wondering what it was like to fly and soar like that. Geese flying south in October can fly long distances without landing.

Fall brought a change in the cornfield, the early frosts turning the leaves brown and the harvesting had already started.

Page 98

Chapter 29

The harvested corn brought memories of winter and the fun we had in the snow and ice, sliding down our hills on sleds, snowballing and ice skating.

I walked to school late in October. I purposely cut across lots that took me to the far end of John Sawyer's cornfield back of the school house. Walking between the rows of corn twice my height gave me the feeling of being in a big forest. Recalling being lost in a field like this as a small boy made chills run up my spine. Whistling as I strolled along changing rows occasionally to get in line with the school house, I heard the "code" crow call. I answered in like manner locating the gang in minutes. I was amazed to find five of my friends under a make-shift lean-to shelter made of dead poles dragged in from the hedge and thatched with dried grass. Dried grass was also used to make a comfortable floor to lounge on under a four foot roof.

The boys were all smoking their pipes. Percy was quick to explain to them that he had invited me to be one of the gang. Percy went to some detail showing me how to make a pipe, not knowing I had already made one. This prompted me to show my handiwork and I proceeded to fill the bowl with corn silk. My first try almost ended in disaster. I got my match burned extra good, held it over the bowl and began puffing away. The corn silk immediately went out of control burning my eyebrows before Percy grabbed it and rapped it out on a stone. Everyone left the shelter believing it might go up in smoke. We went back to the shelter as Percy located some not-so-dry corn silk and loaded my pipe. Lighting it on my second try was successful and I finished the experience with considerable smoke in my eyes and fits of coughing.

Deep notes from the big handbell could be detected above the rustle of dry corn leaves in the wind -- another school day was about to begin. We quickly rapped the pipes and having forgotten a paper bag to put it in, I decided my dinner pail was the safest bet. We avoided unnecessary attention by entering the school playground at different locations and times. I avoided contact with anyone, conscious of my smelly clothes as I put my dinner pail away and hung up my coat and cap and slid behind my desk. The warm, unvented school house intensified the odor, bringing fumes from under my desk like those from my father's smoke house.

Before the teacher called us to order, Helen, occupying the desk in front of me, turned around dishing out some idle talk to make conversation. My reply in like manner brought a look of puzzlement to her face and she said, "Stephen, your breath

Smoking

is terrible. What have you been doing, smoking or something?" The teacher called us to order, so I didn't have to reply. Helen's accusation brought me closer to reality --- fully realizing that I not only smelled like a smoked ham but I had a bad taste in my mouth. I felt an urgency to correct it so I wrote a note to George who always carried "Sen-Sen" in his pocket. I wrote the note, folded it, put his name on it, and started it on its way by our school "shuttle service." It was passed under the desks undetected with no loss of motion until it reached its destination. Soon I had a neatly folded paper filled with tiny black squares of good tasting breath perfume, "Sen-Sen." A few of these improved my self-image for the time being.

The shorter and cooler fall days made our lean-to less comfortable for our occasional smoke, but we continued without thought of giving it up. One day, during morning recess, we noticed that John Sawyer had started to cut the corn and put it in shocks. Even though it was cut one hill at a time with a corn knife, bundled in the arm, tied with twine and put in the shock, one man could cover much ground in a day. I was looking for Judge and found him and read his troubled mind. I followed him around the school away from everyone. As soon as we were out of hearing range, he said, "We'll meet under the big oak tree in ten minutes." Approaching the big oak tree, I saw Judge standing on a big stone with his hands folded like an Indian Chief waiting for his warriors to assemble. Without fanfare or hesitation he began, "Mr. Sawyer will have the corn cut up to and maybe past our lean-to by this time tomorrow. What are we going to do about it?" "I say tonight!" was Percy's answer, "Its moonlight and it won't take long." After a short discussion we agreed to meet at the lean-to at seven o'clock that night to tear it down and throw the poles in the hedge. The school bell cut our meeting short, but we had finished our business, thanks to the boys like Judge who could make quick decisions.

That night after mother had finished the dishes, she said, "Lew, there's enough fire in the kitchen range to pop corn." Dad answered by laying his newspaper down and going to the kitchen followed by my little brother, Earl. Having popcorn with mother's spy apples was a ritual carried on by my dad and my brother a number of times a week. While I was eating corn, watching the clock and

Chapter 29

thinking about an excuse to leave, the phone rang our ring (a long, two short and a long). Ma answered it and said, "Percy wants to talk to Stephen." I nervously answered, mother leaning against the wall with outstretched hand to hand me the receiver. I grabbed it and said, "Hello. What do you know?" "Not much," Percy replied, "How about you?" I replied that I hadn't done a thing. Percy said, "My father told me the township had come up from one cent to two cents on a bounty for sparrows. How about taking our burlap bags along and hunt sparrows in the strawstacks on the way home after we take the lean-to down." I said, "Great!" Percy was at the house in minutes. We bundled up, shouldering our sparrow bags as my father waved a gesture of approval and we stepped out into the night air. The full moon and a cloudless sky cast our shadows as we stepped at a fast pace, anxious to get our job done. All members of our gang got there about the same time, and without ceremony, pulled the poles apart and stacked them in the hedge row. It was

all done in minutes and everyone left to go back home. Having decided not to hunt sparrows, Percy and I walked leisurely home enjoying the beautiful night. I said, "Do you think anyone outside the gang knows about our lean-to shack?" "Oh, I think some do." "How about our teacher, Miss Clark?" "I don't think she knows about it, but she could. You sound worried about it." "No," I said, "I'm not worried, but I can't help but wonder." Then I told him about what Helen said about my breath. Arriving at home, I found Earl in bed, the fire was dying down in the heating stove,

Smoking

and Dad was bringing in wood to stoke the fire for the night. It didn't take us long to prepare for the night, having mother listen to my prayers and crawl into my feather bed.

During the next few days we watched the standing corn succumb to the corn knife and emerge a field of shocks in neat straight rows. Remnants of the lean-to were visible to those who recognized the thick mat of dry grass and furrows left by dragging the poles. We wondered what Mr. Sawyer and his hired hand thought as they cut corn around it. Traveling about the field undetected was no longer possible, so we found other ways to get together and smoke.

We met under the big oak tree and settled on the corn shocks even though they would only accommodate two at a time. Our plan was to work our way along the hedge and cross over to the nearest corn shock without being seen. As we moved to the nearest end of the field, I found myself with George. "Let's take that first shock." I agreed and we climbed under it with George at my side. We parted the stalks at the base of the shock that led us into an opening large enough to hold us both. Stripping some dry leaves from the stalks made us a dry floor to sit on. The wall of the stalks all around us served to fight off the cold fall wind and with pipes lit we had it made.

Things at home and school seemed to be routine for a number of weeks. I was busy doing chores, cutting wood, and checking on the muskrats in the river in preparation for winter trapping. The muskrat "houses" were big that year and the farmers were predicting a cold winter. That week in school had seemed to go rapidly. By Friday night I was already looking forward to a good weekend. After the end of the day, Miss Clark had us already dismissed with books put away, wraps on, waiting for her to say good-bye. I was half thinking about what I had planned to do Saturday and Sunday when her words struck my eardrums like claps of thunder. "I'm dismissing all but Percy, John, Stephen, Judge and George." I immediately sensed it was the corn silk smokers she had in mind. All my blood seemed to go to my head. I put my head in my hands with my elbows on the desk. My fingers registered my rapid heart beat on my temples. I felt sick and glanced at Judge. He managed to grin, but it seemed false. A quick scan at the faces of the kids not involved showed expressions that speak louder than words.

Chapter 29

Miss Clark dismissed the other pupils. We heard the typical parting words from her. When the last kid closed the big front door, we heard loud boisterous voices and uninhibited laughter of children that soon faded into the distance. Miss Clark adjusted the stove damper, then bringing her big book to her desk, totaled her week's attendance record. The quietness of the room was depressing to the point of almost being unbearable. I was especially conscious of the crackling of the wood stove and the rattling of the windows in the wind. We had never had to communicate by facial expression only and I wondered what the others were thinking. Judge, generally thought of as the wisest and most mature by his peers, had all the appearances of one in deep thought. Percy appeared apprehensive, constantly shifting his position at the desk. John, the stoic kind, sat looking straight ahead with a strictly poker face. George acted as though he didn't have a care in the world and he made me nervous. He might start to walk out and upset the apple cart.

I was in a state of shock. I was now sure of the cause of our detention, but not knowing the nature of our punishment, left me feeling insecure and dejected. The thought of what my mother and father might think bothered me most. "How did I ever get mixed up in this?" I thought, and I was filled with remorse and regret.

Attendance records finished, Miss Clark had George place a work table in front of our desks, then she stood in front of us for a moment as if to collect her thoughts. The moment seemed like eternity. She started by saying, "You boys have been smoking in the corn field for weeks and you have set a poor example for the young children and given your school a bad name. I want Percy to come up here." After Percy stood by the table, the teacher said, "Empty all your pockets on the table." Oh, No! For Pete's sake, I thought. She covered our smoking episode in detail with unbelievable accuracy. Where on earth did she get all of this information, I thought. Does she have an informer? Are there tattle-tales in our school? My mind searched for an immediate solution. Where can I hide my pipe? The teacher could search my desk. I quickly recognized my fate.

George was next and he was loaded. I couldn't believe pockets could hold so much. The stench of his pipe reminded me how strong they could get. Each of us went through the same ordeal filling the table with what could have been the biggest display of home made corn pipes ever on exhibition.

Smoking

Before we had time to wonder what would become of the table and its contents, Miss Clark opened the stove door and had each of us throw our own stuff in it. I watched my own pipe alight on the red hot burning embers and turn to ashes.

With the last of the junk in the stove, Miss Clark seized the poker and drove home the hot stove door, then came and stood erect in front of us. She represented both Judge and Jury. We were at her mercy. I prayed silently for leniency. We sat still and motionless wishing she would get on with it, but she was deliberate, seemingly in no hurry. Her slowness irritated me, giving birth to rebellious ideas that were never carried out because we had respect for our teachers and elders. I was a shy person and avoided any conflict rather than have it out with a teacher. I felt wretched with my thoughts of letting Miss Clark down. I recalled her patience, thoughtfulness, consideration of our wishes in the past, and I thought that she always had been fair with us. After seeming to weigh her thoughts, Miss Clark shifted her position, sitting on the end of one of the desks with one foot on the floor. She said, "You boys have been a great disappointment to me. I am surprised you would let your folks down by sneaking out and smoking behind their backs. If I can't trust you, you will remain in school during your recess and noon hour until Mr. Sawyer draws the corn off the field." She then arose from the desk and with an air of dejection said, "You are dismissed."

We left the school without communicating with one another in any way. Outside the school communication was limited to formal "see you tomorrow" and with a simple wave of the arm we left for our individual homes. Percy and I were half way home when he said, "How come your pipe wasn't in your dinner pail?" "It made my sandwiches taste like half burned cobs, so I put my pipe in my pocket. What are you going to tell your folks, Percy?" "Not a thing!" he said, "What are you going to tell your folks?" "I've been thinking about it and haven't decided."

Reaching home, mother met me at the door, as she often did. "What kept you so late in getting home from school?" Mother's friendly, warm and sincere personality always melted me like butter. I always knew it was a mistake to keep anything from her. Then, I impulsively blustered out, "I got caught at school smoking corn silk." Mother didn't appear surprised. She just sat down and I took a chair in front of her. "You already know?" I asked, and she nodded in the affirmative. "Did Miss Clark tell you?" She answered, "Yes." "Do you know our punishment?" She said yes to all my questions. I might have known. I didn't have to ask how Mother and Dad felt -- I knew.

Chapter 29

Dismal depression and gloomy days followed inside the school while others played outside. Checkers, dominoes, tick-tac-toe and other games took our time, but fast became work. Weeks went by with no signs of Mr. Sawyer drawing corn. Desperation brought action. We decided to see Mr. Sawyer and offer to help him draw his corn and get it out of the field. We set Saturday as a meeting time, then drew cuts to see who was to go and arrange a time to meet him. George and I having drawn the short straws, stopped to see him Saturday morning. Mr. Sawyer was a neighbor and a widower. I felt very comfortable around him, but the nature of this meeting made me extremely nervous, putting me under a massive strain. We found him in his barn feeding his cattle. "Hi!" he said as we walked through the door. He seemed surprised to see the two of us at the same time, but realized we wanted to see him about something of special importance. "Let me feed the cows first and I will be right with you."

Mr. Sawyer, living alone, was known to be rough talking, profane when he was working by himself, but pleasant with other people. The cows fed, he emerged from the feeding barn and plunked himself down on the feed box, his long legs swinging on the side of the box. "What can I do for you boys?" he began. I waited for George to break the ice, but he couldn't get under motion. I figured that Mr. Sawyer would be more willing to help us if he knew the whole story. I said, "Mr. Sawyer, we got caught smoking corn silk in your corn field and have to go without recess and noon hour until you clear the field of corn shocks. There are five of us and we would draw your corn..." He interrupted before I could finish, "Why didn't you tell me before? I'll start tomorrow and I'll have it cleaned in a few days."

Boy, were we happy! We thanked him in an awkward sort of way and offered to help him, but he refused. We walked out of the barn thinking, "what a friend!" The corn was in the barn by Saturday and we were set free again from cob pipes and school house confinement.

Chapter 30

CHRISTMAS AT DARROW SCHOOL

Sleighbells broke through the muffled sounds of our schoolroom on a cold snowy mid-December afternoon. Paul stood to shave a peek hole in the frost on the window with the end of his ruler. I saw an instant smile as he turned and I guessed at what he saw. The sound of trotting horses and the sleighbells by the front door confirmed my guess; it was Mr. Burns delivering our Christmas tree. It was a fun time each year when he brought the tree. We loved this short stubby man's joyful and loud manner and dearly referred to him as Billie Burns.

The door flew open as if caught by a high wind as Billie burst in yelling, "Merry Christmas everybody!" with a chorus of surprised kids coming back with, "A Merry Christmas to you!" Many children, shocked by the sudden unexpected appearance and greeting by Billie, were soon in the festive spirit of the moment. I recall how quickly we changed from an orderly schoolroom into an active gay period. Billie's presence alone was conducive to a gala time. His continuous gestures and constant chatter blended with laughter made him a joy to be around. Billie scanned the front corner of the room, then looked at our teacher, Miss Clark. "Where do you want the tree, ma'm?" She stepped back for a better perspective. "About where my desk is." Before you could say Jack Robinson, Jack Burns, Billie's son and Charles Matson had the desk on the other

Page 107

side of the room. Billie was through the front door and half way to the sleigh when he called back, "I want two hands to help with the tree." About ten of us started, but Miss Clark intervened, "He said two." Percy and John were nearest the door and got to help. Billie's conversation with the boys reached our ears. "Put her through butt first, its pretty wide for the door." The three pushed the tree through the door until the lower limbs wedged tight and I heard Billie say "Pull from inside!" Paul and I jumped at the chance to help, grabbed the lower limbs and pulled like we were in a tug of war. The big limbs through the door released the tree suddenly, throwing us to the floor and flipping big hunks of snow from the whipped branches on the little kids and against the hot stove (that made it sputter like grease in a frying pan).

Under Billie's direction we set the tree upright and discovered it was a foot too tall for the ten foot ceiling. "We've got to chop it off," said Billie. So we brought it down flat on the floor. Billie then skipped out to his sleigh, coming back with his axe, and cut the lower branches off the tree, then chopped a foot off the trunk, throwing chips to all parts of the room. Many hands had it back upright in moments. Billie grabbed the limbs and butt of the tree off the floor and threw them in the stove and closed the stove door, but not before the pine needles caught fire and filled the schoolroom with a pine scent aroma.

Miss Clark had a concerned look as Billie drove #8 nails in the window casing to string stovepipe wire to hold the tree upright. Dismounting from his stepladder, he crawled under the tree and asked Miss Clark and the bigger kids when it was plumb, as he shoved the butt on the floor, then toenailed it.

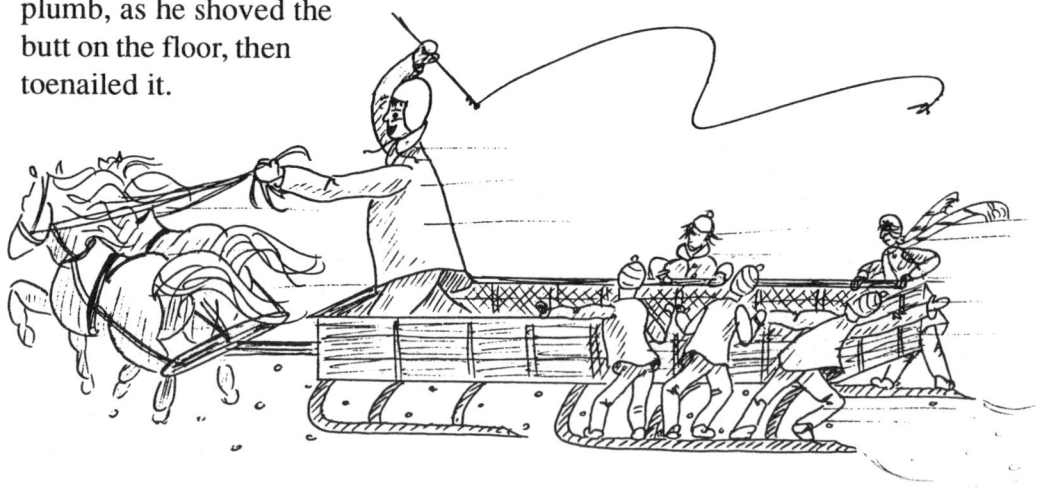

Chapter 30

With a "Merry Christmas" and a "HO! HO! HO!" he left as he had entered, with waving arms and carrying his axe, he got into the sleigh to take off. We big boys had whispered to Miss Clark about riding the runners of Billie's sleigh as we had done before when he had brought us the Christmas tree, so we were all bundled up and out there when he started. He saw us ten-strong coming out of the front door and remembered how in previous years he had tried to throw us off by his crazy driving. We planted our feet on the runners of the bobsleigh with a firm hold of the sleighbox with our mittened hands. We avoided the front bob. If you were thrown off from there you could get run over by the rear bob runner.

Billie had a well matched team of Western ponies about fourteen hands high. They were tough, wiry and instantly obeyed every command given by Billie. Billie first circled the schoolhouse with the ponies close to the building and the sleigh skidded sideways until the back end almost hit the fence. We all managed to stay on until we got to the driveway and turned onto the road when Billie slapped the reins on the ponies, backs and we skidded onto the road. The back end of the sleigh whipped across the road throwing everyone off on the far side of the sleigh, burying them in the deep snow banks. Billie, standing on the front of the sleigh, slapped his hands against his side amused as the boys disappeared in the snow. He reined the horses down the road from left to right until the bob flew from one ditch to the other throwing blinding snow in the faces of those riding the runners. When Billie turned the next corner heading for home, all the boys were strung along the road, buried in the deep snow.

We saw our beloved Billie wave his hand as he drove out of sight, adding to my list of never-to-be-forgotten experiences. We returned to school and were excused by Miss Clark, it being the end of another school day.

Chapter 31

PREPARING FOR THE MICHIGAN EIGHTH GRADE EXAMS

The ordeals and tribulations of growing up and the incessant urge to become an adult and independent made time seem to go at an idling speed. However, the time arrived when I was in the eighth grade faced with a new problem; the Michigan eighth grade examinations. Every eighth grade student in the state was required to pass all subjects with a score of at least 70 as a requirement for entering senior high school. My school work up until then, in competition with my many interests, had not been given top priority. Now, for the first time in my life, I began to assess my year's work in school with genuine concern. I knew that many failed to pass the examination and others chose not to take it, ending their formal education. I began the year with more determination than ever but a horde of activities got in my way, cutting into the time I should have spent on my academic school work. Even though the state tests were the seat of many of my worries and miserable heartaches, I felt they were basically a good idea. Through these tests youngsters didn't get into high school until they had mastered the 3 R's, could think logically and were able to apply their knowledge to every day living situations. There was a good correlation between those who passed the state tests, finished high school and succeeded in their chosen field. However, many of those who terminated their schooling at the end of the eighth grade became good citizens and a few excelled in their occupations.

The passing of the state tests was held like bait in front of all six eighth graders at Darrow School the entire year as an incentive to study. Our teacher was notified in April that pupils from our district would take the test in Albion, twelve miles from our home in early May. In our instructions we were to have five sharpened pencils with erasers, a five cent lined tablet, three steel pens with holders, a tablet of penmanship paper, comfortable clothes and lunch. Our tests would last all day with an hour at noon.

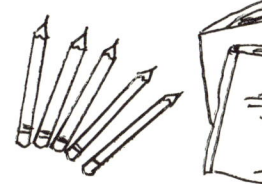

Chapter 31

About two weeks elapsed when Mr. Daniels, our rural mail carrier, reined his horse to a stop on the road opposite our farm shop, where Dad and I were putting a new point on our plow, and called out, "A letter from the School Commissioner came today!" Dad walked out and got the assortment of mail and handed me the Commissioner's letter. Dad promptly busied himself with the plow point as an apparent pretense to hide his anxiety while I opened the letter. "No passing" in three subjects, and the Commissioner's letter declaring I was ineligible for high school came as no surprise. Even though I half suspected a non-passing grade, the definiteness of the letter struck me like a trip hammer on my stomach. I sat on the plow beam and handed Dad the letter. He read it and said, "Many good things come from failure. Time will give you answers." At that time I had one answer to my problem--forget school forever.

That night in our living room by the dim light of two coal oil lamps, my mother and dad told me they had decided to pay my tuition and send me to Homer to school. I accepted it with some reservations, but agreed it was in my best interest.

I entered the eighth grade with Guy Thenon as my teacher. It was bound to be a great year, and it was. I learned more in one year than I had learned in the eight years before. I learned how to study, think logically and reason.

Grown Up

Chapter 32

THE CAR I BUILT

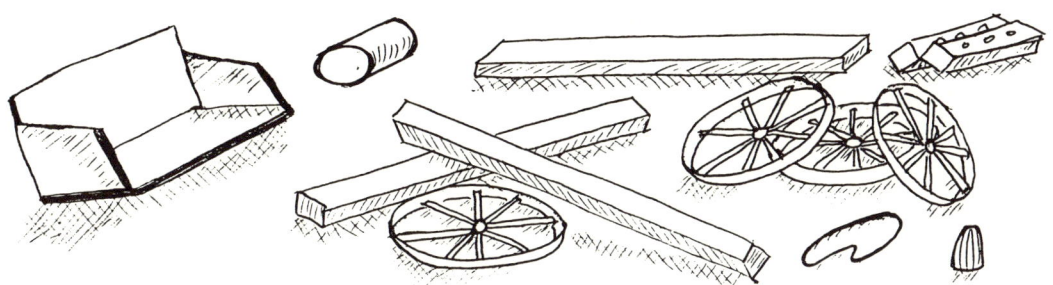

    I made a car before I got through high school. I put a Bosh ignition system on it and a Stromburg carberator, with four cylinders under the hood. It was a Model T and I built the frame out of hardwood. I covered the frame with stove pipe metal and rivited it on. I found a back for it at Ellis Corners. It was square on the back and it made a perfect fit for the part I had already made. I had a door on the back portion so I could throw tools or anything I wanted in the car with me.

    If you bent the wishbone back by accidentally hitting the curb real hard, you couldn't steer it easily and if you tried to drive it you were apt to run into the ditch. Most people with a Model T carried a long bar with them so they could pry the axel forward to get it to steer better. If the wishbone was on the ball and socket end, you had to take it off and hammer it back in shape.

    You could check the oil by opening two petcocks, one above the other, and the oil would run out the lower one and not the upper.

    I didn't have a chance to put a windshield, a top or fenders on until a later date, and only put a door on the passenger side so I could just jump in from my side and drive -- I was young then. I placed a row of buttons in the center of the car and I had to punch them in the right order to get the motor started. I often had someone to crank it for me, but I made sure they kept their thumb outside of the handle before I let them crank it because it would sometimes kick back. It was before self-starters were invented.

The Car I Built

We had a number of floor boards that we could move about and we used to shove them to one side so we could get some heat from the exhaust or muffler during cold fall days. It had no regular brakes on the back wheels but we did have an emergency brake lever to the left of the driver which you pulled back to to apply friction on the back wheels. It was also used for parking.

Three years later we drove the old car to Homer and traded it in on a new Model T Roadster. Before I got there, a valve broke off and went into the piston and when the piston came up it put a hole in it. I came to Homer on three cylinders. They weren't pleased with the car when I drove into the Ford garage in Homer, but they sold me a new roadster anyway. I learned a lesson. I bought it on time and paid a high interest rate. I never bought another car unless I had the cash to pay for it.

We had an experience with the new car we never forgot. We lived in Grand Haven and Marilyn, our daughter, was only a few weeks old. We decided one weekend to drive to Homer because both families lived on farms about three miles apart. We didn't have tinted glass in the Ford, but the light shone in on her in such a way that we thought she had passed out and turned blue. Dee grabbed Marilyn out of the basket on the seat between us and shook her real hard only to find out she was just in a deep sleep. We tucked her back in between us and she went back to sleep. I was wide awake for the rest of the trip.

In the making

drivable

finished

On my Harley

Just married

Off to see the Rockies

Chapter 33

MY INTRODUCTION TO GRAND HAVEN

In April of 1924 I signed a contract to be the first Junior High teacher of Industrial Arts in the Grand Haven Public Schools. The following May I decided to come to Grand Haven along with Francis Drake, who had signed a contract to teach in Holland. We first saw Superintendent Fell in Holland, then came to Grand Haven over a single-lane pavement that required one to turn off on the grass whenever you met another car. We came with a car I had assembled using parts from a number of different automobiles. It traveled much too fast for safety and was truly a mongrel with no windshield or fenders.

We met Superintendent Earl Babcock in early afternoon and he showed us the new High School on Seventh Street, completed in 1922. Later we went across the playground to old Central School. Up until 1922 the third floor of Central School had served as the High School. A seventh and eighth grade Junior High School was established on the third floor in 1922 with Avery Almy as Principal, followed by Glenn Olsen as Principal in 1923-24 and 1924-25. On the way over to Central School I asked to be excused a minute to go to the boys' room. I had started out from Kalamazoo with my best white shirt and tie with the thought of making a favorable impression with my future Superintendent. When I looked into the mirror in the boys' room I was very upset. The lack of a windshield and fenders on my car, driving over dusty gravel roads had changed my clean white shirt a number of shades darker. I quickly washed my face and dried it on paper towels before I left the boys' room. Mr. Babcock then introduced me to Mr. Olsen who showed us around the top floor of Central School. He explained that the old unused Chemistry lab would be used for Home Economics and the Physics lab for Industrial Arts.

We visited a short time when I said we should be starting back for the long trip home over mostly gravel roads. Mr. Olsen walked with us down the three story stairs, out through the storm shed to the circular sidewalk guarded by pipe rails to Sixth Street. Sixth Street had no pavement at that time. Always having lived in the center of the State, I had no conception of Lake Michigan sand. Mr. Olsen said, "Looks like

My Introduction to Grand Haven

your car might be stuck." I replied that I had lots of power and could get out alright. Francis and I got in my car and waved goodbye. I put the car in gear, let out the clutch and immediately buried the hind wheels in sand. Tom Kiel, who lived across the street, Glenn Olsen and Francis pushed like all-get-out, with me behind the wheel, engine racing, until we reached Franklin Street and onto the pavement.

Before we left Grand Haven we drove down Washington Street, out Harbor Avenue and around the State Park. I was impressed with the town but had no idea I would spend forty-three years in the school system there and make the city my retirement home.

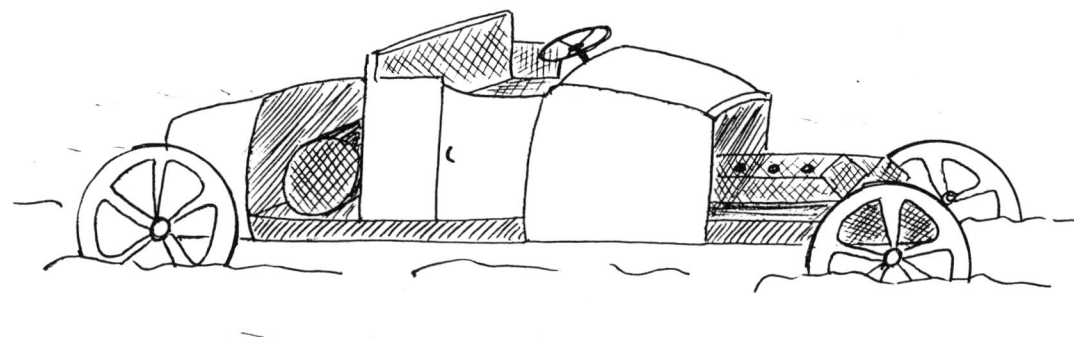

Chapter 34

THE TIME I SHOT THE BULL

We spent the weekend at Pop and Mother McAllister's, Dee's parents, like we often did. I came down on the farm to rest up and hadn't the slightest idea what I was in for. Apparently Pop and Mother McAllister had talked it over and decided to butcher Pop McAllister's bull. I had always done the butchering, so they had an idea maybe I would butcher the bull. They hadn't decided whether to do it themselves or to hire it done by a string butcher. We talked it over and decided to hire it done. He was an ugly critter and had cornered Pop a number of times. Pop got away both times, but each was a close call.

We hired Bill Moore who had a butcher shop east of Clarendon. He had a well-equipped shop with an overhead track that ran the whole length of the shop. He also did custom butchering on the farm, but would rather take the animal to the slaughter house where he had everything to do the butchering. We first had Mill come over and look at the bull. He had many long ropes, a trailer that he pulled with his Ford truck, and a good sized tackle. We finally got a rope on the bull and started pulling him toward the trailer. He smashed against the sides. Mill tried twice more with Pop and I helping, but the trailer ended up kindling wood and he finally gave up and went home with it empty. I think that was the orneriest and ugliest bull I had ever heard of.

We still had a problem on our hands -- shoot the bull ourselves or get another butcher to do it for us. Pop and I talked it over and Pop decided we could do it ourselves.

I didn't have a gun, so I borrowed one from Shisler's, our next door neighbor. It was a twelve gauge double barrel shotgun. They gave us two shells, which we later discovered were old and lacked power. The bull was in the barn between lofts with

The Time I Shot the Bull

sliding barn doors on either side. I had a pretty good shot at him. I whistled at him and, with both barrels of the gun in a cocked position, pulled the trigger and shot him in the forehead as he turned. He just stood and looked at me. I realized at that moment that the shot didn't have power enough, or he would have dropped instantly. While I was looking at him, he held the same position and I shot him the second time. He went crashing through the southern barn door, jumped three fences and ran down the lane. He then jumped two more fences and ended up in Pop's field. I chased him around the field, but decided I was getting nowhere, so decided to do something else.

I then thought of Dave Cortright, who went deer hunting every year, and he loaned me his deer rifle. It was a high powered gun and he said to me before I left, "That gun will carry a bullet about three miles."

By that time the bull was back on Pop McAllister's farm wandering around among some oak grubs. I chased him around for a time trying to get a shot at him.

There was a railroad track that went diagonally through the McAllister farm with a high bank on either side. The bull was running on the inside of the bank so I had a shot against the bank. I took careful aim at his side and pulled the trigger. He dropped instantly and went tumbling forward. I bled him immediately. He was about one third of a mile from my trailer which was hooked onto an Essex car.

Pop McAllister had an old sled and I thought I could haul it on that. I had to go back to get Pop so he could help me. We skinned him because that hide brought three dollars (more if there were no cuts through the hide). That was pretty good money in those days.

We quartered him where he was, otherwise we couldn't keep him on the sled. Besides, without quartering, he would be too heavy to lift. Even then we had difficulty keeping him on the sled. He kept rolling off, plus we had to lift him over a wire fence. It was a blowing day and the wind was from the north, which added to our handicap.

The days were getting shorter and we had to finish with a flashlight and they weren't what they are today. We had to keep shaking the flashlight to keep it lit. We worked until nine o'clock and we had to hang the meat up by quarters. Pop McAllister had to do chores after that, so I helped him. We locked the meat up in the garage so the animals wouldn't get in and help themselves. We had had a long and strenuous day and looked forward to a good night's sleep.

Chapter 35

WATERTOWN, N.Y.

I took my mother to Watertown, New York, when she was seventy years old and we had a wonderful time there. Mother was born on a farm near Watertown. When she was eight years old she left with her parents to come to Burlington, Michigan.

We spent the time in hotels -- motels weren't available in those days. We went to the house where mother had spent those eight years. The couple who lived there then took us through the whole house. Mother saw some things she could remember from her childhood.

We went to the schoolhouse that mother attended when she went to school there. I have a picture of her sitting in the same seat she sat in when she was there as a child.

We went to the old sugar bush where grandpa Chapin and Uncle Leonard (grandpa Chapin's brother) used to tap maple trees and gather the sap in the spring to make maple syrup or candy. Uncle Leonard had been known around Watertown for building stone fences and we saw many of them still standing. They looked like snakes curving over the hills and disappearing out of sight. He would pick up the stones in the field and carry them over to the nearest fence he was building. He laid these fences without mortar of any kind. Each stone was fitted in its proper place to make a fence about three feet high. They had stood for all those years.

Watertown, N.Y.

Uncle Leonard was buried in Watertown. We looked for the grave but we were unsuccessful as it was a large cemetery. I suppose, if we had looked in the directory, we could have found it, but our time was running short.

Thermometers had been manufactured in Watertown and grandpa Chapin had one. You could read it from three different directions. I have it now and I cherish it because it belonged to my grandfather and came from Watertown.

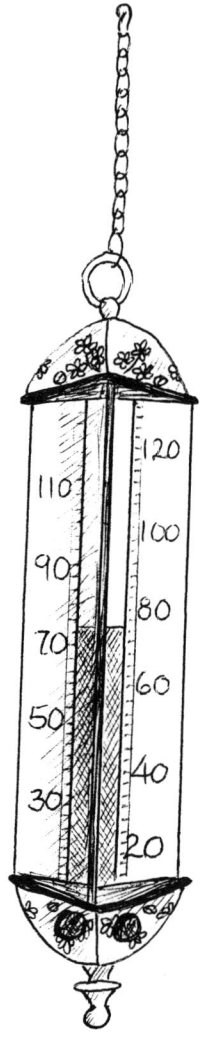

Chapter 36

HOOKED AT HAWKERS

    In retirement we spend our winters in Florida. It's relatively quiet here in the Florida Keys, nothing exciting like Bradenton even though the majority of the people there are retired. Our second day in Bradenton found us well situated and organized so we could take time to do some running around. We both started out with ideas where we wanted to go and needless to say they weren't the same. I had looked forward to going to Hawkers, the most widely advertised and biggest fish market and fishing tackle store in western Florida. Dee had designs on some yellow shoes and I was chafing at the bit to see this reputed magnificent display of fishing tackle. I was driving so we went to Hawkers first. As we passed through the front door my bobber went down -- I knew I had made a find. Dee, realizing my shopping would take considerable time, suggested she hoof it to the shoe store and come back and meet me later. I agreed absolutely as I was in no mood to just skim over this merchandise.

    The store is difficult to describe. It's an old building -- the main room of the store part is filled with fishing gear and a fresh fish counter. To the side is a fishing tackle and reel repair and overhaul shop. That alone would keep one with a mechanical bend occupied half a day. I took a 'pass through' tour at first to get my bearings then started systematically to evaluate what they had that would, in my opinion, keep us in fish while in Florida.

    Quite a bit of time had elapsed when I got to the main plug and spoon display. It was an extensive thing with about twenty-five 3x5 foot panels, all hinged to a post so each would swing and in addition the whole thing revolved. It swung easily as if they kept it well oiled. This permitted you to stand in one place and revolve the panels and swing them from side to side to examine the baits on both sides of them. Characteristic of plug baits, they were loaded with two and three pronged hooks, needle sharp, and some of them had as many as five that would hook a fish if he got within sight of it.

    I thought it was about time for Dee to get back from shoe hunting so I did something against my good judgement -- I started to hurry. One must never let

HOOKED AT HAWKERS

himself get in this state of mind shopping for fishing tackle. In my haste, I stepped in between the panels just as one of those unexpected Florida breezes swept through the building and slapped the panel behind me against my back just as I had both arms up to unhook a plug. I sensed instantly I was hooked -- and good or bad, any way you want to interpret it -- there I was and I couldn't move!! By moving, would it force the barbs deeper into my wool jacket, shirt and undershirt? That was the question. Every instant a little movement of the panel or myself drove more of them clear through to my skin and nerve endings. How I wished Dee would come! I wondered if I should yell for help or start undressing. I thought of buying the panel and walking out with it rather than entertain a store full of people at my expense.

It wasn't long before Dee came and saw me standing there with arms stretched upward so she just waved and started to look at some interesting driftwood. In a minute she realized my pose wasn't just normal and came to my rescue with the famous stock question, "How on earth did you ever get hooked like this?" I replied, "This isn't the first time I've been hooked but for Pete's sake get me out of here!" She took a good look and I knew by her behavior I was in serious trouble. I couldn't make out from her continuous laughter whether it was a nervous reaction or whether she

Chapter 36

thought it was really funny. Then she did the ultimate -- she called to one of the women who worked there. As she approached me she tried to hold back a good laugh but she couldn't. She then called the head man because I guess she couldn't tell what to do with me. When he came over I said, "Who in heck ever designed a display mechanism like this?"

We had a council. I had been in this position for quite awhile and besides I had to go the men's room. I said, "I'm ready for anything -- just tell me what to do!" It was then decided I would either have to go topless and start unhooking each plug one at a time, or get the shears and go to work on my clothes. While this was going on I thought, "Now I know how a King Mackerel feels after grabbing one of these things." As I stood there helpless, Dee and the store woman got my clothes unbuttoned and maneuvered them over my head. It was a painful and hazardous process and I was relieved when freed to go to the men's room. Then, and only then, could I return to help separate the hooks from the cloth.

Some time later, in view of a good sized and changing audience, with the help of my good wife and some store personnel, we got all my clothes unhooked from those wicked hooks and I started out again in a very careful, cautious and serious manner to secure my fishing paraphernalia. It was then that Dee announced she hadn't found her shoes and needed to shop some more and left me alone again (I presume with great misgivings).

Eventually I made my selections and paid for them, locked them in the car and decided to take a walk in the street to cool my nerves after my ordeal, until Dee returned. I got to the first corner on a side street where there was a traffic light but very little traffic, it being around 3:00 p.m. As I stood there, I noticed an old 1959 Chevy approaching the corner at a good clip. The light was turning yellow and it went through my mind, "I wonder if she will try and make it?" She decided to and stepped on it to get through and make a left turn at the corner. As she started the turn I noticed the front right door come open and a white object about 30" long and 18" wide fly out of the car and sail down the street for 25 to 30 feet before striking the pavement. It's velocity and shape caused it to plane perfectly. It made a perfect soft landing and slid on the pavement like a snow sled. As it came to a stop I nearly jumped out of my shoes as I recognized it as a baby strapped in a plastic carrier. I don't know how I got there so fast, just ahead of the manager of a furniture store on the corner. The mother of the child stopped the car so fast that the load of other children landed up in the front seat. She came running our way in house slippers and curlers and grabbed that baby (who was cooing by this time) out of my arms and started back to the car followed by the store manager and myself giving advice, "Take that baby to a hospital and have it examined." As she sped away in the car, the furniture store manager turned to me and said, "Aren't you the one who got tangled up in those hooks at Hawkers?" I looked at him and thought, "Do I have to be reminded of that again so soon?" Then smiled as if I appreciated his concern and replied, "Yes, I'm the one who got hooked at Hawkers."

My Junior High Industrial Arts students in Grand Haven

With my mother in Waterton, N.Y.

Our pet racoon, Mamie

Proud fisherman

Pilot and "co-pilot"

Home workshop

Assembling

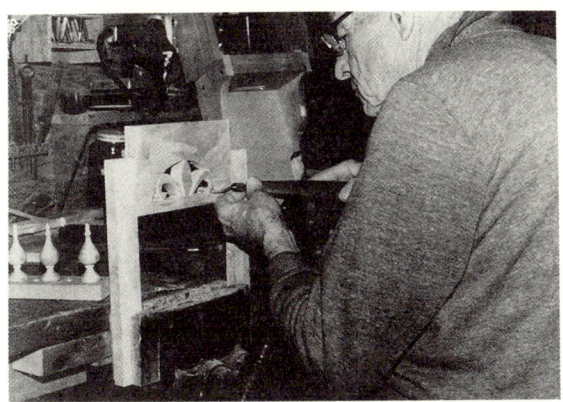

Carving

Completed

About the Author

Stephen Mead was born December 11, 1901 in Homer, Michigan, to Lewis R. and Lillian (Chapin) Mead. He was a graduate of Homer High School and earned his Bachelor's Degree from Western Michigan University. He received his Master's Degree from the University of Michigan in 1938 and did graduate work at Michigan State and Northwestern Universities.

He married Delia McAllister on June 25, 1924, and the couple moved to Grand Haven, where he taught Industrial Arts at Grand Haven Junior High School. He was appointed the junior high principal in 1928 and later served as principal of Central Grade and Junior High School and grade school supervisor.

Mr. Mead was a former secretary-treasurer of the Michigan Elementary Principals' Association and served as president of Michigan Secondary School Principals' Association from 1938-39.

He also served on four state educational committees, including the Secondary School Study of 1938-39. He participated in two "Classroom of the Air" study tours conducted by the State Department of Education and Michigan State University. One included a tour of the major industries of the country; the other was conducted at a U.S. Air Force Base.

In 1948, he was appointed Director of Instruction for Grand Haven Schools in addition to his principalship. In 1953, Grand Haven Junior High School moved to the old high school and added ninth grade. Mr. Mead was appointed Assistant Superintendent in 1959.

He was a member of the Michigan Education Association for 42 years and was a member of the National Education Association for almost as long. He was instrumental in organizing group information of Haven School, which later became the Haven Foundation.

He was a member of the board of directors of the West Michigan Children's Center and was elected chairman of the board in 1949. At the time of his death, he was a member of the board of the West Michigan Mental Health Clinic.

Mr. Mead received his pilot's license on June 22, 1946 and was chairman of the Airport Study Committee appointed by Mayor Wildt in 1943. The airpark opened in 1949, and Mr. Mead served as chairman of the Airpark Board until 1951 and as airpark manager until 1962. He remained a member of the Grand Haven Airpark Board at the time of his death.

Mr. Mead was also a charter member and past president of the Grand Haven Kiwanis Club and was Past Lieutenant Governor of District 11 Kiwanis in 1947.

He was also the first scoutmaster for Troop #5 of the Methodist Church and was a holder of the Silver Beaver.

He was a member of the United Methodist Church of the Dunes where he served in many capacities of the church and sunday school including church school teacher and lay leader.

In addition to his wife, Delia, he has a daughter, Marilyn, a son-in-law, Wallace Van Stratt, 5 grandchildren, and 9 great-grandchildren. His son, Jack, was killed in the Korean War.

Stephen Mead died August 12, 1992.